PANTHER
AND OTHER STORIES OF
GREAT HUNTING RETRIEVERS

DUCKS
UNLIMITED
Memphis, Tennessee

Art direction by Michael Todd
Book design by Lisa Malone

Published by Ducks Unlimited, Inc.
John A. Tomke, President
D. A. (Don) Young, Executive Vice President

ISBN: 1-932052-14-3
Published September 2003

Ducks Unlimited, Inc.
Ducks Unlimited conserves, restores, and manages wetlands and associated habitats for North America's waterfowl. These habitats also benefit other wildlife and people.
Since its founding in 1937, DU has raised more than $1.6 billion, which has contributed to the conservation of more than 10 million acres of prime wildlife habitat in all 50 states, each of the Canadian provinces, and in key areas of Mexico. In the U.S. alone, DU has helped to conserve over 2 million acres of waterfowl habitat. Some 900 species of wildlife live and flourish on DU projects, including many threatened and endangered species.

Call to Action
The success of Ducks Unlimited hinges upon each member's personal involvement in the conservation of North America's wetlands and waterfowl. You can help Ducks Unlimited meet its conservation goals by volunteering your time, energy, and resources; by participating in our conservation programs; and by encouraging others to do the same. To learn more about how you can make a difference for the ducks, call 1-800-45-DUCKS.

Distributed by The Globe Pequot Press, P.O. Box 480, Guilford, CT 06437-0480.

CONTENTS

CONTENTS

INTRODUCTION

The eighteen tales in this collection portray the special bonds that form between man and dog when engaged in the common pursuit of hunting waterfowl and upland game. In many cases, the authors let us in on conversations spoken, as one of them puts it, "in the language of the heart." It's not talk, after all, but "conversation" in the oldest sense of the word, which means living together and sharing common bonds. And it's a testament to the depth and breadth of their individual talents that these fine writers have managed to capture—with words—something so intimate and elemental as this connection between hunter and retriever.

When legendary *Time* magazine reporter Sandy Smith first brought the book's title story, "Panther," to us, we knew we had something special. The size of the story, however, presented a problem. Too short to make a viable book, the little gem was also too long to run as a magazine feature. In the end, we decided to build an anthology around it.

Panther, after all, seemed to embody what every hunter wants in a retriever. A small pheasant dog from the Dakotas, he had a heart as big as the outdoors. If he was too eager for the field-trial judges of his day, his hunting partners and trainers saw this energy for what it was—a burning desire and passion for retrieving that couldn't be extinguished.

INTRODUCTION

Like the legendary horse Seabiscuit, Panther's story is that of an underdog beating the odds. His ultimate triumph, however, was not that he became the most consistent winner in field-trial history. It was in his coming full circle to live out his last days as a hunting dog, pushing pheasants before a boy and an old man, with no one to care whether he broke when a bird flushed.

Like Panther, Sandy Smith has come full circle too. A Westerner, he moved to Chicago as a young man and got into the game of journalism, launching a career that eventually took him to the pinnacle of his field. As a reporter for Time magazine, he had a reputation for being one of the best investigative journalists in the country. As David Halberstam writes in his book on the American media, *The Powers That Be*, Smith was, "second only to Woodward and Bernstein, the top digging reporter on Watergate."

Retiring from *Time* in 1997, Smith returned to Montana, where his heart had always been. He returned to tossing bumpers to his Labrador retrievers, to bird hunting in the fall, but the bug of journalism soon bit him again. As an amateur dog trainer and field-trialer in the late 1940s and early 1950s, he had run into a spitfire Lab whose story had always intrigued him. That dog, of course, was Panther. Smith made a few phone calls and tracked down Panther's trainers…and the rest is for you to discover in the pages that follow.

I mention all of this only because Smith is emblematic of the other writers who have contributed to this book. I can't delineate them all here, but you can find their brief bios in these back pages. Many of them you will recognize as old friends. All of them share a love of the hunt and a deep and abiding appreciation for working retrievers. All of them, too, are humble folk who write in spare and elegant language, allowing the tales to unfold naturally, like a conversation between friends.

Most of these stories are new, written especially for this anthology. Others have appeared previously in print but still seem as fresh and vital as ever.

—Art DeLaurier Jr.
Memphis, Tennessee

1

PANTHER

by Sandy Smith

A small dog with a big heart, Black Panther was the Labrador retriever of his time. At the age of two, he was a field champion. For the next seven years, he was a rocket across the field-trial circuit, picking up twenty-four wins to gain 172 championship points, the gold standard for Labradors. Decades after an eye injury forced him from competition (in 1953) his name led the roster of high-point dogs.

The World Series of retriever trials licensed by the American Kennel Club (AKC) is the winners-only stake held every fall to determine a national champion. Seven times, Panther's wins qualified him to run in the nationals, where he was known as the dog to beat.

What happened to Panther in the nationals was revealed recently by his professional trainers, Orin Benson, now eighty-nine years old, and M. W. "Snuffy" Beliveau, in interviews before his death in 2002.

❧

ONE

The Wild West spawned many outlaws. Among them, in 1945, was Panther. At the age of nineteen months, he was a forty-seven-pound bundle a natural ability. He had taught himself to retrieve under the guns of hunters in the Dakotas. When a flock of pheasants, driven from a cornfield, flared into flight as the shotguns boomed, it was up to Panther to bring in the dead birds and chase down the cripples. The only thing the hunters taught him was his nickname, Triever.

His crew of admiring shooters soon got the notion that Triever, whose formal training was a point zero, might do well in big-time field trials. But Panther's owner, Charles Cutting, was a man of modest means. His Dakota liquor store was barely profitable. He could not afford the field-trial entry fees. No problem, said the gunners, each dropping a few bucks into a pot for Panther's entry into three stakes.

Three weeks later, Panther, his owner, and the posse of fee donors traveled to the trial grounds at Fargo, North Dakota. All were entirely unprepared for a contest with strict etiquette and protocol as rigid as appellate court procedures. One rule, they discovered quickly, was inflexible: the retriever must be "non-slip." That is, the dog must remain motionless or "steady" until a judge calls its number. Only then can the handler order the dog to retrieve.

Panther and Cutting were called to run. At a signal from the judges, gunners in the field shot a pheasant.

Non-slip? Steady? Numbers? Fuhgeddaboutit!! Panther took off.

In two stakes, he was eliminated for "breaking" when the shots were fired. In the third test, Panther didn't wait for shooting. Spotting the gunners, he ran out to them, prancing and whining, as if imploring them to shoot the birds. Again, of course, he was eliminated.

Panther's outlaw performance was shocking to the field-trial crowd, but Cutting's faith in his dog was undiminished. Cutting sought out professional trainers, hoping some pro might be willing to take Panther at a bargain rate in the belief that the dog would eventually win. He spoke with a Wisconsin trainer, Charles Morgan, who rejected Cutting's pitch as a bad gamble. Pointing to another dog trainer, Morgan said, "That guy over there, his name is Benson. Talk to him. He might help you."

Cutting went over to Orin Benson. As it turned out, Benson had done more than just watch Panther. He recognized raw talent when he saw it. "Your dog has a lot of fire," said Benson. "Harness that energy and you'll have a winner."

Cutting made it clear he was broke, telling Benson that he could not pay anything for training and that he might be unable to scrape up enough cash for the entry fees. Why not? Benson reasoned. What have I got to lose? He told Cutting, "Pay what you can. I'll take him, work with him, and see what he can do."

ONE

That agreement, with a handshake, put Panther on Benson's truck. Panther rode back to the Benson kennel and into field-trial history.

The early days at Benson's place near Eagle, Wisconsin, were critical for Panther. "I knew what I had and what I had to do," said Benson, who has trained animals from bulls to timber wolves. "I had to steady Panther and keep him from breaking before I could do anything more with him."

Yet he recognized that Panther was "high strung" and that heavy-handed tactics—such as beatings to keep him steady, or check cords to stop him dead when he was moving at high speed—might dim his burning desire for birds. So Benson trained him with a very light touch. For hours Benson kept Panther sitting while other dogs retrieved dummies and dead birds. Panther sat again as pigeons were shot for other retrievers. If Panther budged while another dog was working and the command "No!" didn't stop him, Benson used a slingshot to nick his hindquarters with a marble. "When he was steady, I praised him and gave him dog food treats," said Benson. "He was smart. He caught on fast."

Cutting's order to retrieve—"Go get 'em boy"—was changed, of course. Benson sent Panther by calling his nickname, Triever. Before that command, on a marked bird,

Panther was on his own. "I never gave Panther a line [a direction] on birds he saw fall," said Benson. "On multiple marks, I'd let him decide which bird he wanted first."

Benson was scornful of the force-breaking system of teaching a dog to retrieve to hand. "There was none of that with Panther," he said. "He'd come in fast with the bird. You had to be quick, like a shortstop fielding a hard-hit ground ball. Panther would almost spit the bird at you. It might be hard to catch, but that was his style."

During training and later in field trials Panther sensed when he had done things right. As he walked at heel with Benson after a good performance, Panther would leap into Benson's arms to show his affection and celebrate a job well done.

A cash customer paying monthly bills might have objected to the cost of Benson's happy-dog training. But Panther's owner, Cutting, wasn't paying a cent for Benson's services. That gave Benson the luxury of bringing Panther along slow and easy, without protests from the owner.

Less than a year after Panther's outlaw performance at Fargo, Benson brought him to the competition level of field trials. Only one hitch remained—the immediately disqualifying fault of breaking. It was a hard-to-forget relic of the

ONE

Dakota pheasant drives, when nothing delayed Panther once shots were fired and a bird tumbled to the ground. At a trial, if a bird were downed close to him, Panther was always on the verge of breaking. "I worked Triever on a lot of birds—pigeons, ducks, and geese, dead and alive," said Benson. "But never on pheasants. In training, I tried to keep Panther away from that temptation. At a trial, though, when pheasants were shot, he was ready to go. Sure, most of the time I could keep him steady. But not for too long."

In September 1946, Panther won his first open all-age stake. A month later, he placed second in another trial to qualify for the 1946 National Championship at Crab Orchard Lake in southern Illinois. Of the twenty starters, Panther and two other dogs were eliminated at the end of the fourth test.

In the following year, 1947, Panther won seven more field trials. And the passing of more than fifty years has not dimmed the recollection of Panther's flashing style in the memory of former field-trial judge F. Robert Noonan. "I saw Panther the first time at a Wisconsin trial," said Noonan. "On a shot bird, most dogs slow down a bit to pick up the pheasant or duck. Not Panther. He never broke his high-speed stride to snatch up the bird. He came in the same way, at full throttle. 'That's some dog,' I told Benson."

Noonan recalls that Benson, who was bold enough to needle a judge when he was running a dog as good as Panther, said "Oh Yeah. But he doesn't like the water."

A water test came next. According to Noonan, "Panther hit the water like a black torpedo. I said to Benson 'You told me he didn't like water.' Benson joked, 'I meant he didn't like to drink it!'"

Panther's wins in 1947 attracted the attention of Carl Carlson at a time when Cutting was seeking cash to open a new venture in Montana. Carlson was looking for winners, but he knew very little about field trials. His offers for young dogs were turned down by several owners before Carlson began bidding for Panther. Cutting was willing to sell for the right price.

Their serious dickering began in October at a field trial in Billings. At the end of the first day of the trial, Carlson made a then-astounding offer of $5,000. Cutting took it, although he and his wife were in tears at the prospect of giving up Panther.

The field judge, John Fraser, was selected to draw up the contract. One clause gave Benson the right to train and breed Panther for the next five years. "The two men asked me what I thought about the deal," said Fraser at the time. "I told them it was a bum deal for them both. They wanted to know why. I said I didn't figure that any dog was worth that much and if I had one that was, I'd keep him for myself."

The next day, Panther's first test was a double marked retrieve—shot bird on the left and, far out in the heavy cover, a pheasant that had only been crippled by the gunners.

Fraser, the judge, told Benson: "You don't have to take that long bird; it's a runner."

"He [Panther] saw it," said Benson. "I'll take it."

Panther quickly collected the short bird and set out for the cripple. He trailed the running bird across a stream and up a hillside, where he caught it. The pheasant was still alive when he brought it in to Benson.

Panther's win at the Billings trial was his sixth in 1947. It was the first trial for his new owner, Carlson. As the trophy was presented to Carlson, Panther licked his face. Carlson—who was so happy he wept—said, "If I paid $20,000 for Panther, I wouldn't have paid too much."

As might have been expected, the sale of Panther drew press attention. It was reported as a rags-to-riches saga, with Panther—as a Cinderella—sold by the weeping Cutting to Carlson who, shedding tears of joy, shelled out a sum that, in the 1947 economy, would have bought a small house or a big car.

It might have been better for Panther if all this had been kept secret, or at least private. For such tabloid notoriety was distasteful to the field-trial crowd, a mix of Wall Street financiers and wealthy sportsmen whose dogs retrieved driven pheasants and flighted ducks at private shooting grounds on the East Coast. Some figures in that Long Island high society were members of the National Retriever Field Trial Club that stages the championship trials. Another was a member of the AKC board. Still others appeared as judges at the national trials.

In the fall of 1947, Benson loaded Panther and other dogs into a Chevy truck and drove east for the trials on Long Island, the cradle of field trials in the United States. Carlson tagged along, determined to break through the upper crust. As Benson recalls it, Carlson lugged along several sacks of silver dollars, each bag weighing in excess of forty pounds.

In the watering holes of Sag Harbor, Carlson tossed a bag of silver dollars on the bar and, waving to other field trainers, ordered the barkeep: "Give those guys a drink!"

The bar was silent. No one would drink with Carlson. The chill continued the next day at the trial—a second-place ribbon was all Panther picked up on Long Island, described by Benson as the wellspring of animosity against Carlson.

But Panther's seven wins in the West earlier that year had more than qualified him to run in the 1947 National at Crab Orchard Lake in southern Illinois. Twenty-one dogs started that trial on December 5. At the end of the ten tests required by the rules, four dogs remained in the running. Two were handled by Benson: Black Panther and Black Roland of Koshkonong, also known as Dusty.

To the East Coast field-trial gentry Dusty was as scary as Panther. Panther's owner was rich, to be sure, but still just a plumber. Dusty was owned by Wesley Jung, who worked for a farm equipment manufacturer in Fort Atkinson,

ONE

Wisconsin. A lifelong duck shooter, Jung named his Labrador after a Wisconsin lake that was a haven for canvasback ducks. Nothing much elite in all of that. To make matters worse for the East Coast faction, Black Roland had come close to winning the 1945 National Championship on the elistist home grounds, Long Island.

The other Labs in contention after ten series of the 1947 national were Bracken's Sweep, owned by Daniel E. Pomeroy, founder of the Banker's Trust Company in New York City; and a three-time national champion, Shed of Arden, owned by Paul Bakewell III, of Saint Louis. The judges were J. Gould Remick, a member of the board of the AKC and chairman of its retriever advisory committee; Thomas E. Merritt, a member of the AKC advisory committee; and the Michigan field-trial judge, F. Robert Noonan.

As the tenth series ended, Benson and the late T. W. "Cotton" Pershall, the handler of Bracken's Sweep, concluded that the trial was over. Pershall's opinion, according to Benson, was that the winner was one of Benson's dogs. "Thinking the trial was finished, Cotton and I went back to our trucks to prepare food for our dogs," said Benson. "When the judges called for extra series, Cotton told me: 'I don't know why they're doing this—your dog already won it.'" According to Benson, Pershall didn't say which dog, Panther or Dusty, was the winner.

It was a Catch-22 situation in which the three judges ordered more tests, hoping to reveal a weakness in one dog that would give another a clear victory. After two more tests, the trial ended with the announcement by the judges that Bracken's Sweep, owned by Dan Pomeroy and handled by Pershall, was the 1947 National Champion.

A short time later, Judge Remick approached Benson to offer advice from the supremes. "You're young," Remick told Benson. "Your time will come. Dan [Pomeroy] has done so much for field trials. Your time will come." To Benson, those words sounded like an apology.

The last word in the 1947 championship controversy came later, from Pershall. Pershall and Benson were side-kicks as well as competitors. Their friendship began in field trials and continued until Pershall's death. "Whenever we talked about that 1947 national," said Benson, "Pershall told me the same thing. 'Orin, you got screwed.'"

Benson believed that both of his owners, Carlson and Jung, were unacceptable to the East Coast field-trial peers. And so Pomeroy's Bracken's Sweep became the national champion.

Benson's dog truck in the late 1940s was loaded with Labrador field-trial champions. The heavy hitters included Panther, Black Roland of Koshkonong, and a dog named Mully Gully Goo. Mully's owner was John Sturtevant, a

Wisconsin newspaper publisher who had lost his voice to throat cancer. Sturtevant used handwritten notes to communicate with other people. Communicating with Mully was more difficult.

All retriever handlers use arm gestures to handle dogs in the field. It is necessary to stop the dog with a whistle before giving him an arm signal to go back, left, or right. But Sturtevant, with his voice gone, couldn't blow a whistle.

Benson solved that problem. He slipped the bulb of a turkey baster off, and fastened the bulb to a whistle. By squeezing the bulb, Sturtevant could blow the whistle. And that ingenious device enabled him to handle Mully at field trials.

At a Wisconsin trial in 1948, Panther and Mully were among the dogs in the final test. Panther's previous wins in that year had qualified him for the Nationals, but Mully needed a win to qualify. Baster bulb in hand, Sturtevant was handling Mully in the final series. It was a double retrieve — one bird shot close, followed by a long "blind." (Note to readers unfamiliar with field-trial lingo: In the so-called blind test, the judges and Sturtevant saw a dead bird dropped out of Mully's sight. Sturtevant was then required with whistle and arm signals to direct Mully to the fall of a bird that the dog had not seen.) The day was warm. Sturtevant gave Mully a line to the blind and then stopped him with a baster-bulb toot about twenty yards from the bird. Sturtevant raised his right arm as the signal to go back. But Mully could not distinguish Sturtevant's arm from the other shirtsleeves in the crowd.

Deep in the gallery, Benson groaned at the sight of Mully, tail flashing, looking in vain for direction. The judges knew that Sturtevant was unable to speak, so they gave Mully some time. But both Sturtevant and Mully appeared frozen. Benson could not be silent any longer. Mully couldn't see him, but the dog knew Benson's voice. "Back!" shouted Benson.

Mully whirled and got the bird.

Most of the owners and trainers in the crowd were well aware of Sturtevant's disability. Almost everyone was happy when the judges pronounced Mully the winner. Everybody, that is, except Carlson. Carlson, citing the rule book to the judges, charged that Mully had received illegal assistance. Benson promptly asserted that he had done nothing to help Mully. His account was supported by the owners and spectators around him. And Carlson was unable to identify the voice calling "Back!"

That, the judges ruled, was that. Mully was officially declared the winner and qualified to run with Panther in the National. But 1948 wasn't their year. Mully was dropped after the fifth test. Panther broke in the seventh.

More than fifty years later, Benson remained unrepentant about the Wisconsin trial. "Sure, I hollered 'Back!'" said Benson. "Mully and Sturtevant needed that win. But I think somebody whispered to Carlson that I did it. In the end, Carlson got even. He took Panther away from me."

ONE

In the spring of 1949, Carlson brought in Snuffy Beliveau to handle Panther in California, where Carlson, still irked by the Sag Harbor freeze-out, hoped to gain some acceptance from the laid-back movie colony. It didn't work out that way, however. Carlson was much too square for the movie people. But Panther ran well in the West. He won two trials under Beliveau and placed in two more. Back with Benson in the Midwest trials from May to October, Panther picked up four more wins and other points, scoring every time he ran. "Carlson wanted wins and more wins," said Beliveau. "He wanted so many that other owners were complaining that they couldn't qualify their dogs for the National because Panther was winning everything."

At the time, a dog qualified for the National with one win, plus a single point. But Panther, in 1949, won or placed in every trial he entered. As a result, five other dogs might have gone to the National on the points Panther picked up after he was qualified in 1949. "The other owners had a legitimate beef," said Benson. "Panther did present a problem to them. The problem was that Panther was the most consistent winner in field-trial history."

To cope with the "Panther problem," the field-trial establishment expanded the entry in the Nationals and liberalized the qualifying standards. Some field-trial judges took a more direct approach, devising so-called breaking tests and other snares to eliminate Panther, then running at the senior age of seven. Such ploys were blatant and produced an unexpected backlash. To protect Panther one handler sacrificed his chance to win at a trial in Illinois in 1951.

At the start of that trial, Beliveau suspected that the judges were out to get Panther. The first test seemed to prompt Panther's recall of running out of control in the Dakota pheasant drives. But now, the slightest slip would permit the judges to drop Panther.

Clearly, the initial tests presented double jeopardy. First, a pheasant was shot thirty yards deep in a field of standing corn where Beliveau couldn't see Panther. Next, a blind was set on the edge of the cornfield. To get the blind, Panther had to be lined and handled along the edge of the field where he had retrieved the shot bird. But if he veered back into the corn again the judges would drop him from the trial for going out of control on the blind.

Benson and Beliveau used the same system to handle Panther. The dog selected his own birds on marked retrieves. Only on blinds did the trainers give Panther a line. So, in this field-trial trap, when Beliveau gave Panther a line, Panther apparently understood that he was not to go in the corn again. He took the line, right along the edge of the corn, directly to the blind, avoiding the first snare. The last test in the Illinois trial seemed aimed squarely at Panther's only real fault—breaking. It was a double marked retrieve of pheasants shot close to three dogs on line.

"Panther retrieved his birds without a hitch," said Beliveau. "He was required to honor [remain steady] while the other dogs worked. He sat through one set, but I could see he was getting edgy. On the last set, one of the birds fell fifteen yards from Panther. His hindquarters started to lift—a sure sign he was ready to go. I didn't think I could hold him much longer. But suddenly another dog on line, a golden retriever, charged in for the bird and was eliminated from the trial for breaking."

As he walked Panther back to his truck, Beliveau passed the handler of the golden. "Snuffy," said the other pro, "my dog didn't break. I sent him. They [the judges] aren't going to get the old man [Panther] that way."

Panther was declared the winner of the Illinois trial. In November, he and Beliveau traveled to a place called Carnation, in the state of Washington, to run in the 1951 National. During that National at Carnation Farms, the weather was vile. "All three days, the trial was run [in] rain, fog, and mist," said the National Retriever Field Trial Club history. "It was a rough assignment for judges and trial personnel..."

Thirty-nine dogs started the trial. On the third day, at the end of the required ten tests, Panther and four other dogs, field-trial champions all, were called back for an eleventh test near dusk. It was a double marked retrieve. One duck was shot in the willows along a creek. Another was downed a long way from the creek, deep in heavy underbrush.

In the callback of five dogs, Panther was the fourth to run. But his first bird fell almost on the bank of the creek. The judges called it a "no-bird" because it was too close. In most trials, when judges announce a no-bird, the dog is taken off the line to come back after a few dogs have run— at least three—so that the memory of the old fall does not interfere with the old dog's rerun.

In a similar situation, a judge could scrub the entire test, ordering all five dogs to run again in another location where the odor of the no-bird fall would not tempt any dog.

According to Beliveau, there was time at Carnation to run a fresh test. It could have been run that afternoon or, if the judges were reluctant to risk that, the trial could have been extended to a fourth day. But that didn't happen in the eleventh series of the Carnation Nationals. Another Catch-22 nightmare began to unfold for Beliveau when Panther was ordered back to run the test over the same no-bird ground.

The long and short birds were shot. Panther got the short bird quickly. But when Snuffy sent him for the long bird, Panther scented the no-bird fall and ran along the creek bank, seeking the bird he knew had been there. "Panther was sniffing around for that no-bird fall," said Beliveau. "I had to handle him off that to get him back to the deep bird.

That cost me a National win. I was sad, but I wasn't surprised. It was to be expected. After all, I was running Carlson's dog."

Many flashy winners begin to slow down at the advanced age of seven or eight. Not Panther. In March 1952, at the age of eight, he won in northern California and Oregon. His third win was at Sun Valley, Idaho, when Carlson, still seeking some semblance of social entrée as the owner of a champion, appeared as Panther's handler in an amateur-only stake. "Carlson wanted to demonstrate that he could play the field-trial game," said Beliveau. "He seemed to think—how hard can it be? I tried to talk him out of it but he wouldn't listen. It was a disaster."

Carlson came out with all the props. He traveled from Helena to Sun Valley in a brand-new Cadillac. He wore a snow-white jacket so that Panther could see him at a distance.

When Panther and Carlson went before the judges on a water blind retrieve, Beliveau took a position where Panther could see him and—hopefully—recognize that being handled by Carlson was serious business.

That play didn't work. When Carlson ordered "Back!" Panther trotted out to a small marsh to perform what Snuffy described as "monkey business." Carlson whistled for Panther to stop.

Panther didn't stop.

Carlson whistled again.

Panther ignored it.

Seeing that Carlson could not control his dog, the judges ordered Carlson to pick up his dog. Carlson blew the come-in signal. Panther ignored that, too.

The judges finally summoned Beliveau to get Panther out of the marsh. The other amateur handlers gave Carlson the cold shoulder. No one came around to encourage him to keep trying to handle his champion. Carlson never tried it again.

Panther's seventh and last run in the National was at Weldon Springs, Missouri, in November 1952. Thirty-two dogs started the trial. Panther and ten others remained in the running for the last test. The final series, as Beliveau recalled it, included a bird shot over a multiflora rose hedge studded with thorns. "Some dogs went over the hedge," said Beliveau. "Panther spotted a hole and went through it. He came back with the bird the same way and a thorn caught him in the right eye. When he brought the bird in, I saw that the eye was closed."

At the conclusion of the tenth test, the judges awarded the championship to King Buck, a Labrador. Buck's owner was John Olin, the owner of Winchester-Western Arms Company and the Nilo Kennels in southern Illinois.

Early in 1953, Beliveau had physicians from Stanford University examine Panther's eye, which had become infected. "The Stanford doctors cleared up the infection, but they were unable to restore Panther's sight," said Beliveau. "He was practically blind in one eye."

The eye injury hurt Panther's ability to mark the fall of a shot bird. It also made blind retrieves more difficult as Panther, with vision in one eye, had to turn around completely to pick up a signal from Beliveau. Nonetheless, Carlson wanted wins. So Panther continued to run, half blind, at the age of nine. He ran for three seconds and a third in West Coast trials before Beliveau called a halt. "I couldn't stand it," said Beliveau, an ex-Marine. "It was unfair to Panther to run him with one eye. I told Carlson I wouldn't run Panther anymore. I dropped Panther off at Carlson's place in Helena, when I drove to the 1953 National in Maryland."

Back in Montana in 1954, the irascible Carlson began to learn something entirely new—the joy of companionship with a Labrador. Over the next three years, Panther taught Carlson a lot about that.

When Beliveau dropped off Panther with an admonition to keep him out of field trials, all Carlson really knew about Panther was restricted to a display of his trophies.

To be sure, it was impressive—a glittering array of sterling silver bowls, winners' rosettes, and oil paintings in a

showcase that filled the entire north wall of Carlson's second-floor condo in Helena.

To his credit, Carlson took the first halting steps toward
bonding with Panther. He had seen Panther leap into the
arms of Benson and Beliveau, so he gave that a try. Opening
his arms, he called, "Triever." Panther vaulted onto his chest
and nuzzled Carlson under the chin. Panther knew just how
to capture an owner. Carlson was hooked on the spot. From
then on, according to Carlson's grandson, Don Hurni, the
old man regarded Panther as the most important thing in his
life. The showcase remained, but only as evidence of
Panther's accomplishments.

Before Panther's age and eye injury forced him from field
trials, Carlson spent hours each day in a Helena brokerage
office watching the stock ticker. Now, for Carlson, playing
with Panther was more rewarding than playing the stock
market. He built an elaborate kennel with concrete runs, calling it Black Panther Kennels. Then he recruited his grandson
to toss dummies and birds for Panther in the fields around
Helena. Both Panther and the boy were twelve years old.

Next, Carlson set out to scrub the humiliating memory
of his attempt to handle Panther at the Idaho trial in 1952.
Then, Panther and his owner were strangers. Now, Panther
recognized Carlson as a pal. To the grandson, it was miracu-
lous. Panther began to give some heed to Carlson's whistle
signals. It wasn't non-slip or field-trial stuff, but Grandpa was
actually handling Panther, more or less.

In the fall, the old man and the boy went hunting behind the high-point dog that had slipped the bonds of field trials. It must have been something to see. Free at last! When Panther broke as a pheasant flushed, nobody cared. No supremes were around to announce a "no-bird" if a crippled pheasant took off on the run. Panther was half-blind but he still had a nose. None of the cripples got away.

"Carlson really didn't care, then, about shooting a lot of birds or a perfect performance by Panther," said Hurni. "Carlson was proud of Panther, period. That was more important to my grandfather than bag limits or field-trial style." Late in the game, it seems, Carlson discovered that winning wasn't everything.

As he turned thirteen, Panther's fires were burning low. His rocket pace had slowed. He had to be helped onto the tailgate of a pickup truck. In the spring of 1957, he was unable to mount the stairs to Carlson's second-floor condo. For a time, Carlson carried his champion up and down the stairs. Next, it became difficult for Panther to walk at all.

The end came on July 8, 1957, when, as Carlson described it, Panther "was put to rest." In a letter to editor John Fraser, at the *Retriever Field Trial News,* Carlson wrote that he had acted "to relieve Panther of any suffering." Carlson told also of the gift of joy he had received from Panther. "I don't know where a man, at any price, could find more joy than I had with that little fellow," Carlson wrote.

Stung by the news, Fraser wrote back that, to him, Panther "exemplified every attribute of a great retriever," adding: "If ever anyone had to eat his words, I did after I told you at Billings I thought the bargain was a poor one for you and 'Chuck' Cutting. You nor no one else [sic] will ever see another Panther, but I do hope you will find some consolation in the knowledge that you owned and had as a companion the greatest."

How Panther was put down is unknown. Carlson's enemies in the field-trial crowd spread the word that Carlson had ended Panther's life with a shotgun blast, a common practice at that time. Another grisly tale, offered by a former field-trial judge, was that Carlson tossed Panther's corpse on a garbage dump.

But Carlson's grandson believes that the old man asked a vet to give Panther a fatal injection. He recalls that an urn with ashes rested on top of the trophy showcase after Panther's death.

࿇

Author's Note: For many years, retrievers were ignored by the Field Trial Hall of Fame at Grand Junction, Tennessee. But the hall was expanded in 1992 to include retriever champions and high-point dogs in a Retriever Field Trial Hall of Fame. Two more years passed before the retriever hall got around to recognizing Panther, in 1994. And for two years after that, Panther stood alone in the hall with no mention of his trainers.

The hall finally admitted Orin Benson in 1996. And Snuffy Beliveau? He has yet to make it.

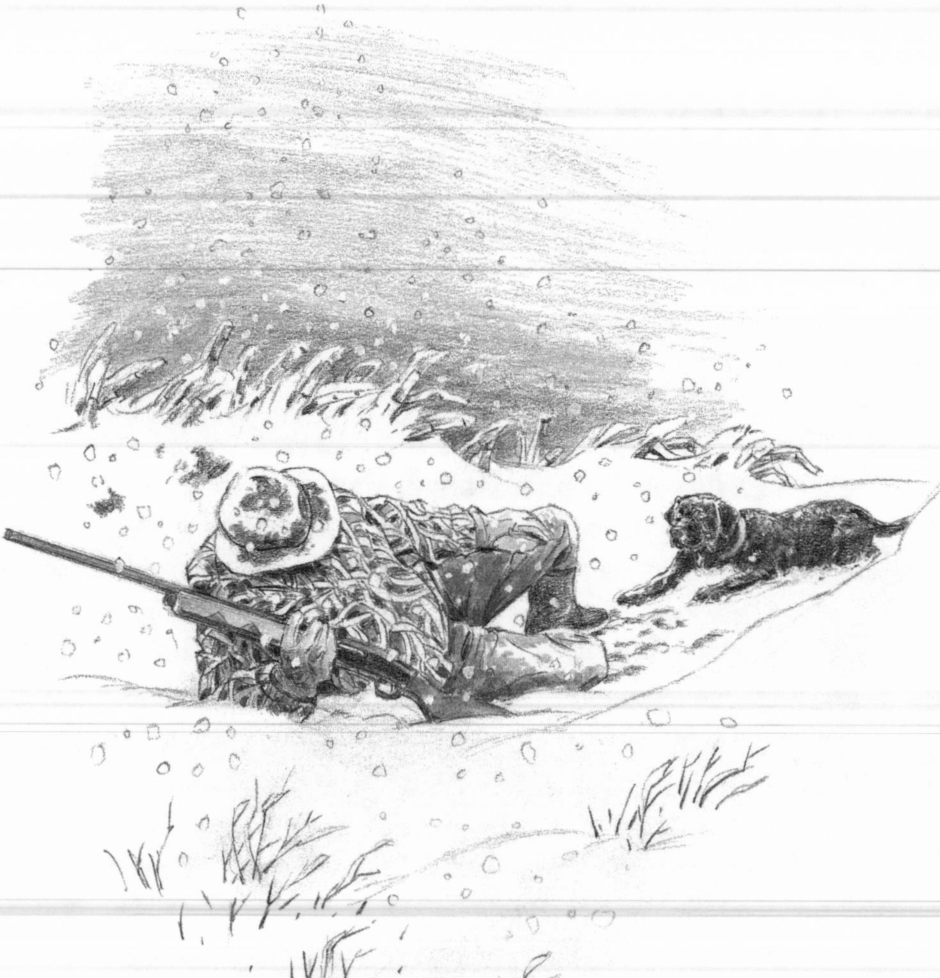

A ROUGH-SHOOTING LABRADOR

by Joe Arnette

The bedroom was awash in soft, autumn moonlight when I awoke, gradually drawn from sleep by a sense of being watched. I turned my head slowly, at ease with what I would see, and looked into the eyes of a dog: deep and richly expressive eyes that I knew, even in my half-conscious state, mirrored a comforting blend of concern and unqualified devotion.

Perhaps, while asleep, I had done something that caused him to sit up and move close—his muzzle was just inches from my face—then stare at me with a uniquely canine focus. Maybe my breathing had slowed, or tired muscles had twitched, or I had muttered dream words. Or more likely, considering the dog, checking on my well-being was part of his nightly routine—a routine that had gone on for years, but only occasionally awakened me.

Whatever the reason, a moment after I turned my head and our eyes met, he nuzzled my hand, stretched his neck slightly, and licked my cheek. In turn, I finger-stroked his jaw and whispered, "Good boy." At the sound of my voice, satisfied all was well, he sighed and dropped into his place, bathed in a pool of moonlight, at the bed's side.

He was a Labrador retriever—big, blocky, and night black—and I called him Buck. By no means an unusual or original name, but one that fit both my Lab and my needs. Like many other gun-dog owners, I was attracted by the name's simplicity, lyricism, and the implication of greatness recalled from a youthful passion for Jack London tales. But unlike other hunters, I had saved "Buck" as a term of endearment and as a symbol of expectation for a special dog—a dog I judged would be singular. And I was right in that judgment of my one and only Buck: I hadn't used the name before him, and I haven't used it since.

What made this Labrador different from other dogs I've owned was not overwhelming good looks, sweeping skills, or exceptional élan, but a quality of extraordinary allegiance that commonly took away my breath. Toward the end of our second season together, I began to understand that Buck's greatest talent was his moment-to-moment drive to always be involved with what I was doing, to carry out what I asked of him, and, in some cases, to anticipate what he thought I intended to ask of him. At a point early in our relationship, however such things occur, he had decided that I was his reason for existence. And he never deviated from that decision.

Like most of his breed, he was content to be with his people—in this case, with his person—and was tolerant of all
that went on around him if I was part of it. He would sit
patiently in front of me and watch me, completely attuned to
the tone of my voice, as I spoke to him of my troubles. Deep
into nights he would lie stretched by my chair, eyes cocked
upward, waiting for the last drink to be finished, the last
friend to leave, the last word to be spoken. Only when I was
safely tucked away would he fully relax and take his own rest.

If I took a midday break from pheasant hunting and
dozed on a warm hillside, he would be there when I awoke.
That he would stray did not cross my mind. During a slow
morning in a duck blind, I could snooze without fear that
when I opened my eyes the decoys would be on the bank,
chewed and line-knotted. When ducks were in the air, a
whine announced their presence or, if it was needed, a
nudge brought me to my senses.

And all he asked in return for such full-time fealty and
dedication to duty was to be there, and to receive a scratch
and a smile now and then. But there was more to our
involvement than an occasional kind word from human master to canine servant. For a good many years he was my
hunting partner, guardian, unknowing confidant, and, in a
way explicable only to those who have had such a relationship, my friend. After his arrival in my life, it did not take

overly long for us to become extensions of each other, at least as much as man and dog can achieve that state.

Buck was born in the Southeast, sojourned in the Midwest, and spent his peak years in the Rocky Mountains. He adapted equally well to each of many residences, restrictions, ventures, and forays into—for him—new and unknown worlds. As long as we were together, it seemed that high chukar country was as good as a coastal duck marsh, and rooting roosters from swamp edges matched gunning geese on western waters.

Certainly Buck's early background played a role in his affinity for people, his attachment to me, and his often amazing ability to focus on my actions of the moment. He had been hand-reared—nursed, nurtured, and socialized—the result of a mammary gland infection that almost killed his mother. His breeder spent long, arduous hours caring for the sizable litter. This devoted woman lavished all possible affection and attention on the pups. And her concern didn't stop when the time came to sell the litter.

The passage of years has not dimmed my recollection of the grillings she put me through to determine my suitability to own one of her dogs. For a small-time breeder like herself, she told me, money was not the sole point; where she placed each pup was the main issue. She produced a litter of her Labradors only once every year or two, and most pups went to professional trainers. I have no idea why the woman decided that I should have one of her pups, but she lived by her words and sold me a dog at a fair price.

Although she gave me my choice of the remaining pups, she picked up a squirmy, pink-tongued bundle of black fur and said, "I've been dealing with this litter constantly for nine weeks. I can't tell you why, at least not in a way that would make sense, but I think this is the puppy you should take." Then she placed the pup that would be Buck in my arms and added, "It's up to you."

Did the breeder experience a serendipitous moment before she handed me that particular pup, and did I apply greater-than-usual common sense in accepting her choice? Or was it a typical puppy-selection crapshoot—given a similar rearing, would another male from that litter have turned out much the same? In truth, the why of how I came to hold a certain pup doesn't matter; what counted then, and still does count, were the results.

I've owned dogs that had wider-ranging skills than Buck, or that were superior to him at individual tasks—more aggressive brush-busters, cleaner markers that ran harder lines, stronger and more stylish retrievers. But for all-around, hunt-anything-at-anytime competence and for day-in, day-out performance, my rough-shooting Labrador retriever, Buck, remains unmatched.

I've always liked the term "rough shooting," in part because it is without pretension and is perfectly descriptive of a particular style of hunting. Mainly, though, I'm drawn to the words because I've done so much of what they define so well. Although I was primarily a waterfowler, for a lengthy stretch of my life I hunted everything feathered and furred that was legal and even marginally available. I hunted constantly, in all weather and on all terrain, and I considered anything that moved on that diverse terrain to be fair game. I didn't know it at the time—I was poorly versed in classic sporting literature—but I was a rough shooter with all of the implications, both good and bad, inherent in the term. And Buck was my rough-shooting dog.

Now, tagging a dog with the rough-shooting label doesn't imply a lack of skill, drive, or even polish. At least in my mind, rough shooting hints more at the unimportance of rigid structure and formalized etiquette, and suggests a certain laissez-faire style of hunting. In keeping with that style, during his peak years Buck found, flushed, tracked, and fetched an astonishing array of game. He wasn't going to win any titles as a national-caliber performer, but he brought a jack-of-all-trades finesse to each hunt. He showed up for all of the jobs I asked of him, no matter how bizarre they might be, and he was damned good at getting them done. Over and above day-after-day workmanship, during my benchmark years with Buck he displayed a flare for inventiveness and, on occasion, brilliance.

Cw

Meteorologists probably have a technical term for weather that can't get much worse, but "beyond rotten" is accurate enough for me. That was what I thought of the midmorning weather that had descended rapidly on my makeshift blind. Although it likely took at least an hour for conditions to disintegrate to beyond rotten, it seemed that one moment the skies were standard November gray, while the next a front had stormed out of the north, dropped over the mountains, and blanketed the valley. Freezing rain came first, followed by a mixture of sleet and wet snow. Then the temperature plummeted and thick snow slanted in on a driving wind. Visibility fell to fifty yards at best.

Buck and I were hunkered down in a toss of driftwood backed by a spread of reeds along the edge of a river backwater. The river was fair-sized, well over one hundred yards wide at certain points, but serpentine as it looped through the thirty-mile length of valley floor. Some of these river loops, or oxbows, had created a series of substantial backwaters that, over time, had become mini marshes. And if there was enough land between oxbows, local ranchers planted grain crops—mainly corn—crammed to little more than a combine's width from the water's edge.

Behind my driftwood hide, the riverbank inclined sharply upward for about ten feet to level off onto one of those cornfields, desktop flat and harvested down to stubble. Earlier in the season, resident waterfowl had regularly used the combination of river, backwater, and cornfield. Although Canada geese drifting through the valley soon learned that this could be a dangerous practice, I could count on enough duck flights into the backwater to keep most mornings interesting.

When the storm struck, I had three mallards beside me in the blind. The first bird had decoyed perfectly just after Buck and I had settled into the driftwood. Minutes later, the other two drakes had ripped over the rear of the blind, flying wing-tip close to each other. I had taken a questionable, long shot and had hit both birds. The pair had wobbled on another sixty or so yards, then fell together into the backwater.

One-hundred-yard, marked retrieves—even doubles— are small peanuts on the upper echelon field-trial circuit. But in a duck marsh laced with channels and interspersed with reed beds, mounds of thick brush and dead trees, and other obstacles, such pickups are not simple affairs for a shorter-range, working retriever.

Buck had made a fast job of the first mallard, but had strayed off-line going back for the second bird. When he was about seventy-five yards out, he stopped swimming and climbed onto a mound topped by the stark trunk of a drowned cottonwood. He stood there for a moment, looking back at me, before turning and staring at the backwater.

Then something clicked; he hit the water again and went unerringly to where the mallards had gone down. Within minutes, Buck was offering me the second bird. Even with his glitch—given that I had not handled him—to my eye it was a nice piece of retrieving work. And I spent some time telling him so.

I had gotten the three mallards shortly after sunrise, but hadn't seen a bird since, not even on the far horizon before the storm hit. Nor had Buck, though he was ever alert, on the lookout, and adept at spotting in-comers. However, with the rapid change of weather from typical to terrible, I assumed ducks would be mobbing the smaller, protected backwaters along the river.

The mob turned out to be a single drake gadwall that materialized out of the snow and immediately dropped into my decoys. Buck sat immobile, leaning forward and locked onto the duck puddling among the iced-up, snow-covered blocks. I was collecting my gone-numb legs under me to stand and take the gadwall when Buck's ears cocked and his head tilted up and to the side. Then I heard them. Canada geese. They weren't talking much, and what noise they made was muffled and dispersed by the wind, but it sounded like they were closing on us. I glanced at the gadwall as he slowly moved through the decoys and disappeared into the snow curtain hiding most of the backwater.

The geese, ten to fifteen of them, were quiet when they went over the blind, huge and looming, not twenty-five feet above the top of my snow-crowned hat. They appeared, then they were gone—enveloped again by the cloak of white over the cornfield. After a burst of gabble, the only sound was the wind. They had gone down in the corn stubble close to the river's edge, of that I was certain.

I stood, stamped my feet, and beat snow from my jacket. Buck followed my lead, shook snow and ice water from his coat, and waited for orders. If a dog is capable of a dismayed expression, Buck had one when I commanded him to stay in the blind. I intended to put a sneak on those geese—I felt confident they were less than seventy-five yards away—and even with the advantage of wind and blowing snow, I didn't see any way a big dog could remain undetected in the approach I was going to use.

The shallow irrigation ditch was at most two feet deep with a scattering of weeds along its edges. But it bisected the flat cornfield, and I was reasonably sure that a low crawl—slow and patient—would bring me close to the geese. Before I eased up the riverbank to make a hunched-over sprint to the ditch, I glanced back at Buck sitting in the driftwood—his look had progressed from dismayed to forlorn. I gave him a reinforcing hand signal to stay put, then headed out.

For the first twenty yards of my crawl, I was so focused on keeping my butt down and my gun muzzle up that I ignored what sounded like low, nasal snorts behind me. I thought they were noise from wind gusts until it registered that they were rhythmic. I rolled onto my right shoulder, looked back, and saw Buck low-crawling up the ditch—chest and belly pushed into the snow-packed bottom, front feet pulling him forward, hind feet shoving him along. For a moment, lying in that wet, iron-cold furrow in the earth staring at my dog, I was doubly dumbfounded. Buck rarely disobeyed a direct command; but more than that, I had neither taught him how to crawl nor seen him try it.

Most dogs, if they had ignored a command and followed, would have simply run up or along the ditch. But not Buck. I believed then, as I do now, that his actions were pure imitation—he watched me crawl up the ditch, then mimicked exactly what I was doing. I scowled at him, but stretched back my hand to touch his head. When he nosed my glove, I knew that his world was again in balance. The dual low crawls began again.

The upshot of this singular sneak was that we crawled within twenty yards of the flock. I killed one goose that fell in the corn stubble, and solidly hit another that floundered over the river, barely above the surface, making for the opposite bank. I sent Buck quickly, just as the crippled bird vanished into the wall of blowing snow. Although he had fixed on the goose when it was hit and had a good line on its flight, there was no way of knowing how far the bird would fly and where it would come down. Also, he was swimming a wide section of river with a muscular current that would push him off his mark. I gave Buck little chance of making the retrieve.

I watched him plunge into the wind-chopped water and swim an inky line rulered along the path where he had last seen the crippled goose. When he disappeared into the blanketing white, I collected the dead Canada from the stubble and returned to the point on the riverbank where Buck had entered the water. I crouched there to wait, huddled into as small a wind-and-snow target as possible.

Twenty minutes brought second thoughts about the wisdom of sending Buck under such conditions. After another fifteen minutes had gone by, I was at the water's edge whistling "Come back" as loudly and frantically as I could. And then I saw him—or at least I saw the vague darkness of his head largely hidden by the gray-black lump of goose—swimming hard but tired and low in the water, halfway across the river about thirty yards downstream. When he heard the whistle, he turned in the water to swim toward me, but along with carrying the goose he was fighting both the chop and the current and couldn't make headway. I ran down the bank to shorten the swim and get him out of the water.

I'll never know the details of that retrieve. But it was, undeniably, monumental. More than a half hour had passed between Buck's disappearance into the snow and his reappearance out of it, meaning he didn't simply stumble over the goose lying on the bank. Whatever happened on the snow-cloaked, opposite shore, Buck had to track and find the bird in a driving blizzard, then back trail to the point on the bank where he had left the water. He had to have done that; pure luck cannot account for the reality that, on his return, the river's current had shoved him no more than thirty yards off-line from where I waited.

I dispatched the goose, then led Buck to a washed-out section of bank that offered a bit of protection from the storm to let him rest before we pulled the decoys and headed home. We sat in the lee of the wind, snugged against each other. When I wrapped my arm around his wet body, he sighed heavily and laid his head on my knee.

As a fitting conclusion to that day—on our way to the truck, fighting a slightly diminished wind—Buck paused, thrust out his head, and flared his nostrils; then he moved toward a marshy sprawl of brush and cattails between the cornfield and the end of the backwater. Early in our seasons together, I had learned to stay alert when Buck got birdy. False alarms were not his style, and this time was no different.

I knocked down the first rooster as it sailed up and over my left shoulder. The bird tumbled dead in the stubble. A moment later, Buck flushed six more pheasants; four hens flew low over the cornfield, while two roosters caught the wind, arced high above their brush and cattail hideout, and headed for the backwater.

I'd like to say that I deliberately targeted the second rooster, though in truth I went for the lead bird. With the power-
ful tailwind propelling them, I was at least ten feet behind the
leader, but centered the follower in an explosion of storm-
whipped feathers. The wind and the bird's forward momentum carried it well into the backwater.

Buck's retrieve of the second rooster, though his mark
on the bird was obscured by snow, was routine, like many
others I'd watched him make. But as he left the backwater
and topped the bank's earthen shoulders, then trotted to me
through the still-vicious storm and sat to deliver the bird, I
felts tears on my cheeks. There was something universally
expressive in the flow of images—Buck's weary gait, water
freezing on his fur, the way he held his head and the bird,
the rooster's tail tip dragging the snow, with its feathers in
wind-blown disarray and fluttering over the Lab's eyes.
Perhaps it was a combination of those things, or a culmina-
tion of the entire morning, or a summation of all the hunts
on all the mornings that had gone before. Or it could have
been the biting wind that caused my eyes to water. But I
don't think so.

Not only did my rough-shooting Labrador, Buck, play a
feature role in an important chapter of my life, but also, in

many ways, his presence defined it. Although the seasons have written that chapter's final page, I can revive its contents at any time and in any fashion. To be sure, a remembrance of things past has equal meaning whether it is of yesterday or yesteryear, whether it is glimpsed as a hazy, subtle vignette or revisited as a long, pleasurable reminiscence.

Indeed, I can conjure pieces of that life chapter with Buck at will, as a mind's-eye vision of a dog appearing out of blizzard to deliver a tail-dragging rooster, or that same dog fighting a seething river with ten pounds of Canada goose in tow. And, yes, I still see a Labrador retriever—big, blocky, and night black—bathed in a pool of soft, autumn moonlight as he sits by my bedside and watches over me.

BESS' STORY

by John Madson

L arry Reid stopped by a while back, as he often does when he's got a new duck call. A new old one, I mean. He's afflicted with galloping collectivitis for vintage wildfowl calls, which isn't a bad way to go considering that they tend to appreciate in value, take up less room than a decoy collection, and never need dusting. Wives notice things like that—and a duck hunter can do with all the wifely goodwill he can get.

Settling down in my boar's nest of an office, Larry led me through the labyrinth of events that had resulted in his most recent acquisition—a battered walnut tube that was highballing mallards when Harding was president. The account of this odyssey lasted nearly as long as Harding's term of office.

At last the yarn was spun, the antique duck call slathered with praise, and a reflective pause entered the proceedings.

"Reid," I observed, "for you, duck hunting is just an excuse to hunt junker duck calls."

"That is base calumny," he replied stiffly. "There's nothing I'd rather hunt than ducks. Especially when there's a bonus."

"Like another old duck call?"

"No, better than that..."

And away he went, again.

When things are right, the Batchtown Flats are a glory hole. A broad embayment of the Mississippi behind the Winfield Dam in southwestern Illinois, it's a thousand-acre duck haven of smartweed, millet, mudflats, and open shallows.

On that November day, though, things were not right. Comes to that, things couldn't have been much worse. Bluebird weather—clear, warm, quiet. The kind of day when Batchtown hunters have been known to fish for crappies from their blinds. At the Batchtown check station, there had been a wishful rumor that a new flight of ducks was on its way—but no one put much stock in that. Not with the forecast of a day in the balmy 60s with no weather fronts up north to push anything southward.

But you go hunting when you can, and Larry and his gunning partner, veterinarian Art Lippoldt, figured that hanging around a duck marsh beats hanging around town. Which, of course, it always does.

And so they headed out to their blind on Turner Island, a maze of shallow sloughs and marshy potholes in the middle of the Mississippi, a half-mile west of the Batchtown Flats. Not once in the two-mile run to the island had there been any sign of ducks. The big island had seen a lot of red-letter days in the past, but this wasn't one of them. Not at first, anyway. "Which just goes to prove," Larry said, "that you never know about duck hunting."

He and Doc set their spread of seventy-five decoys and sat back with pipes and coffee, contemplating smartweed beds and quiet waters that remained steadfastly duckless.

Doc had his female black Lab, Windy, as usual. They came as a set. Larry had his black Lab, Bess—one of Windy's pups from six years earlier. Bess was swollen and miserable with a false pregnancy of the sort she often had after a heat period, but Doc assured Larry that the condition wasn't harmful, just uncomfortable. "I almost left Bess at home that day," Larry said, "but she sweet-talked me out of it. She wanted to go hunting so bad."

Full sunup, and still no sign of ducks anywhere in the sky. Then, Larry remembers, "The flats seemed to explode."

The eastern sky suddenly was skeined with ducks, newcomers that began working the decoy spreads in spite of the guns. Poultry all over the place—but not over Turner Island. There, peace and serenity reigned under a blue and empty sky.

THREE

Still, you hang around, never knowing when a few scraps might fall off the table. From out of nowhere, a lone mallard drake swung over the decoys in easy range. Larry took the shot, and Bess hit the water to fetch the day's first duck.

An hour later, two drake mallards and a hen came in off the river, answered the calls, and set their wings. Larry and Doc each dropped a greenhead, the birds were neatly retrieved, and tranquility again settled over their blind. Off to the east, it still sounded like a Juarez election. Through Doc's binoculars, flight after flight of ducks could be seen settling into the flats while our two heroes languished under an empty sky as a hundred other guys were having powder fits less than a mile away.

It was more than any duck hunter could endure. Something had to be done even if it was wrong. In late morning Doc said, "Some of those guys are bound to have killed out by now. One of us should go back to the check station and see if we can get a blind over there in Hog Heaven…"

Doc won the toss, and Larry made the run to the landing alone. When he drove his pickup into the check station's parking lot, one look at the traffic told him the trip had been for nothing. As the flights of new ducks had come pouring in, the word had gone out and local hunters were waiting to take over hot blinds where limits had been filled. Larry joined the crowd, but at almost noon he was still twelfth on the list.

Enough of that. "Take my name off the list," he told the officer in charge. "I'd rather be out there on Turner Island taking my chances than messing around here."

He took his time going back. Why hurry? There were ducks throughout the flats—but still none in sight around the island. He hid the boat and walked over to the blind where Doc was grinning the big hello.

"What are you so happy about?" Larry growled.

"Before I let you in," said Doc, "you have to guess what's in the blind that wasn't here when you left."

"OK. So how many did you kill?"

"I got three blacks," Doc replied.

"What? I'm back there sweating out a line while you're sacking some black mallards?"

"Who said anything about ducks? Look at this."

On the floor of the blind lay Larry's Bess, with three black puppies no bigger than dressed teal. Soon after Larry had left, Bess had begun scratching under the seat of the blind—and once she began whelping, she made steady progress.

"She's had two of 'em within the last half hour," Doc explained proudly. "No problems, though. When you told me about her false pregnancy, I didn't pay much attention. This would have made the fourth time in the last two years, right?"

Right—except that Larry suddenly remembered the summer weekend when he'd attended a drawing for blind sites. Some of the hunters had brought their dogs and one big male Lab, in particular, had seemed smitten with Bess. *A-huh...*

"What are we going to do?" Larry asked?

"Just let nature take its course," Doc replied, "and keep hoping for ducks. No sense in moving her and the pups as long as everything keeps going as it has so far."

At that point, a lone drake almost knocked their caps off. Doc dropped the greenhead just beyond the decoys, a cripple. "Grab your dog!" he said. "We don't want Bess to get wet!"

Larry seized a black neck with one hand and opened the door to the dog ramp with the other. Off and away went the Lab, with a surging splash.

"Reid!" yelled Doc. "You've got hold of Windy! That's Bess after that duck!"

No whistling or yelling could turn the gallant Bess. Lunging through the shallows, spraying mud and water widely, she finally caught the mallard when it became tangled in heavy smartweeds seventy-five yards from the blind. Bird in mouth, she trudged heavily back to a warm welcome.

Doc was bent on keeping the pups as warm and dry as possible. A perfect solution was at hand. Three of the mallard drakes and an old towel were arranged on the roof of the blind to form a nest in the warm sun and dry willow branches. It's doubtful that any swamp dogs, anywhere or anytime, ever had a more suitable welcome to the special world that would honor them and which, hopefully, they would honor in turn.

"They nestled into those greenheads as if they were try-ing to retrieve them," Larry said. "And about then, pup num-ber four arrived…"

So did more mallards—a christening gift from the Red Gods, some old hunters might say. As if drawn by the mew-ing puppies, ducks began coming out of the clear November sky in singles, pairs, small bunches. For the next hour or so, there was no thought of anything back in town, and the most important family problems were those being presented by Lady Bess. The dog chute had to be carefully guarded and blocked, for every time the hunters sounded their calls, Bess would be up and ready to go. As a fifth greenhead was added to the bag, a fifth puppy was added to the little nest on the blind's roof. Soon there was a sixth puppy. The nest was rap-idly outgrown, but the wherewithal to enlarge it continued to drop out of the sky.

"This has to be some kind of record," Larry said as he moved puppies down into the blind to nurse.

"How so?" Doc asked.

"You ever heard of anyone hunting ducks with eight Labrador retrievers?"

The rest of the hunt was a happy confusion of filling lim-its and tending a half-dozen squirming objects that were as black and shiny as lumps of anthracite. With ten drake mal-lards and six puppies, the hunters decided to call it a day, pick up, and report to the check station.

THREE

That establishment was basking in the sweet, smoky ambience that check stations always seem to have when the Brotherhood of the Drippy Nose has limited out. Grinning hunters with heavy strings of mallards and pintails stood about, still sharing the common adventure and the many marvels of the day. There was far more talking than listening.

With carefully calculated nonchalance, Larry laid out ten mallards on the checking table.

"Looks like you guys did the right thing, going back to Turner," said the biologist in charge.

"You know it!" Doc broke in. "How about that? Ten greenheads and six blacks..."

"Six blacks? Are you crazy? That puts you way over the limit!"

"No limit on this kind of blacks," Doc grinned, and began hauling puppies out of the pockets of his big hunting coat. That shut off every other conversation in the room. It was the hit of the show, being played stage center to an audience of stern critics—all of whom gave rave reviews. Half the puppies were spoken for on the spot. After all, blood will tell—and how can any retriever whelped in a duck blind turn out to be anything but a top dog?

Out in the truck, Bess added pup number seven to the Lab population. An eighth and last puppy would arrive at home.

ᕬᕙ

Larry settled back in his chair, I poured more coffee, and we both reflected in the warm afterglow of a well-told tale.

"A hunt to remember," I offered.

"Deed it was," said Larry. "Sure, Doc and I both remember when there were more ducks moving ahead of a northern front, or other hunts with odd twists of luck. Some mighty interesting dogwork, too."

"But I've never seen anything to match Bess' performance that day. It's been over twenty years but I still remember every detail. The way I figure it, the best duck hunts come in three parts: planning, doing, and remembering. I can't say which is the best. Can you?"

"No, I can't."

But if there's anything better than a perfect three-part hunt and eight new Labs, well, Larry and I will keep our mouths shut while you tell us about it.

THE PRICE OF A DOG

by Michael Furtman

W hat is a good dog worth? What price? Can it be measured with coin or currency?

I don't know the answer to that question. But I believe that, like your first love, your first dog remains always special, even though those that follow are loved and remembered for their own special qualities. Although my family had always owned black Labrador retrievers, Gypsy was the first black Lab I could truly call my dog, a dog that came along while I was in college. She was as footloose as I was, a stray that showed up in my sister's garage, eating her dog's chow. Spirited off to the dog pound when no one would claim her, the young stray caught a break when my sister called the day the dog was to be destroyed—her children crying at the very thought—begging me to rescue this wayward retriever.

The dog pound is, of course, not the best place to shop for your next hunting dog. I knew this, but figured that I could

at least take a look. Perhaps I could offer the dog a temporary home, and a reprieve from the gas chamber. For the fee
of $5.25—to the Duluth Dog Pound (DDP) to buy a dog
license—the skinny, mangy black Lab was mine. A bath and
a trip to the vet revealed that not only was she a good-looking dog, but also that she was not as old as I had feared, possibly under nine months. I began to train her immediately.

Perhaps because she had lived on her own for lord
knows how long, and perhaps because she had been abandoned, Gypsy was aloof. It was a trait she never lost, except
with me. She had little time for most other people, but was
devoted to me, attentive to my every word and gesture. I was
young, single, and though dirt poor, free to hunt and fish
when I liked. Together we learned the ways of the woods
and marshes, and spent many nights sleeping in tents or in
the back of the truck. I measured women by how they reacted to my dog, for if they were to have me, they must accept
her. Several fairly good prospects were rejected either by me
or by Gypsy, based on how they reacted to my dog. And that
was just as well. For by being so choosy, this intelligent
black dog encouraged me to remain single late into my twen-
ties. And when she decided that the attractive brunette
woman I brought home was fine by her, I ended my single
life and Gypsy gained a new friend.

If many things changed with my getting married, one
thing did not. Gypsy and I continued to hunt ducks with pas-

sion. She was as good a retriever as I had any right to pos-
sess, and her abilities far outstripped my own as a trainer. She
had faults, as do I, but they were not of her making, but mine.

Her looks were certainly not one of those faults. A female
Lab with the male's blocky head, she was a dark-eyed beauty
queen—so much so that many another hunter inquired
about when she'd be ready to breed with their dog.

One such inquiry came from a man who was the sales
representative of a gun manufacturer. Some twenty years or
so ago, I was the manager of a gun shop. That year, this gun
maker's catalog had some lovely photos of a truly handsome
Lab in it. When I mentioned the pictures to this salesman, he
replied that the pictured dog was his, that his company maintained its own dog kennels, and that because he had been
salesman of the year a few years back, he had won pick of
the litter. That handsome boy dog was his, and he proudly
told me of the dog's exploits.

As well he should. One of the pleasures of owning a dog
is telling tales of it, and so I politely listened and "wowed"
and nodded in all the appropriate places. It seemed he had
good reason to be proud of that dog.

When he finished, it was my turn. Now if you are new to
dog ownership, I must tell you that the rudest thing you can
do is fail to show appreciation for the next person's dog stories. If you are going to have any right at all to tell your own,
you must simply hang in utter rapture on their words, or
you'll forfeit all right to lie or brag about yours.

Which is just what this jerk did. He ignored me as I talked about Gypsy. It was like talking to a gumball machine. I didn't forget it.

The next time this salesman scheduled an appointment to show me his company's guns, I brought Gypsy to work. That's one good thing about gun stores—employees' hunting dogs are often welcome.

After the salesman had finished showing me the year's new wares, and I had written the order, I retreated into my office and returned with Gypsy on a leash. "Geez, that's a good-looking dog," said Mr. Salesman. "How old is she? I'm thinking of mating my male. Your dog looks like a fine prospect."

I said she was four.

"What kennel is she from?" he asked.

"The DDP kennel, right here in town."

"Hmm, I thought I knew all the good kennels, but I've never heard of DDP. Do they have good blood lines?"

I said they have all kinds.

"What did you pay for her?"

"Five and a quarter," I replied.

"Five hundred and twenty-five dollars! Why, I don't think even our kennel gets that much for a good dog. What the heck was the name of that kennel again?"

"DDP kennel—the Duluth Dog Pound. And I don't think your dog is good enough to mate with my $5.25 dog."

He wasn't amused. But I was.

If he wouldn't listen to my bragging, at least I know that, if you've read this far, you will. I appreciate it. So here goes.

ᴄᴡ

Gypsy's most remarkable gift was that of her sense of smell, a sense no other dog I've owned or hunted over has ever equaled. Once, during a snowfall in North Dakota, Gypsy was covering for two blinds a hundred yards or more apart on a long, deep prairie pothole. The mallards and pin-tails poured in through the snow, some meeting death, others escaping to the south. Gypsy and I were kept busy retrieving everyone's ducks, and she fetched more birds that day than many a dog does in a full season.

If you've never hunted ducks in a snowfall, let me tell you that it is a remarkable thing. The ducks appear as if out of nowhere. How they even know that there is water down below when the air is as thick as one of those shaken snow globes I'll never know. But down they drop—brazen chested, feet dangling, and wings cupped—suddenly appearing before startled hunters who rise cold and stiffly, their shotgun barks muffled by the wet air. And so it was this day: both blinds seeing great action, six men relishing the experience, and one very happy retriever.

Once, after cleaning up some downed birds for my friends in the south blind, the dog and I returned to our station in the other blind, only to learn that guys there had been busy, too, and several ducks dotted the water. Gypsy made short work of them and the pile in the snowy blind grew ever larger.

Jeff Nelson, my wise, elder duck-hunting friend, took one look at the most recent retrieved birds and told me that one was still missing. I asked how he knew.

"Because I know I knocked down a fine drake pintail, and there are none in the pile," he replied. "If it was a cripple, it probably swam off into that stand of cattails on the other shore."

Jeff had been hunting ducks longer than I'd been alive, so I never doubted his word. Wondering if I'd ever again get the chance to pull the trigger myself, I climbed from the blind. From the water's edge, I gave Gypsy a line, sending her across the water and into the cattails. Once she hit the far shore, she sped into the dense cover, but almost immediately popped back out. That was quick, I thought, and was waiting for her to begin her return. Instead, she stood at the water's edge, staring at me. Her mouth was empty.

I motioned her back into the cattails, and again she entered but did not hunt dead. Almost immediately, she emerged birdless and stared back in my direction.

One of the things I've regretted in my life is growing angry with a dog when it really didn't deserve my wrath. But I was young and hot with the thought that she was disobeying me. I fired some choice curse words across the water as I grew angry at her refusal to scour those cattails. She just stared back over the water. Finally I decided that it was time to walk around the edge of the pothole and give her what for. We had had several of those kinds of discussions over the years.

Just as I was about to hitch up my waders and march over to the dog, a remarkable thing happened. I noted that not only was she ignoring me, but also she was staring out into the pothole, her head slightly up, her big nose working the breeze. Without a command from me, she eased into the slushy pothole and swam out to the middle, where she paused, treading water.

Now if you recall, we'd whacked a bunch of ducks in this slough, and there were feathers floating everywhere out there. I guessed that she was merely smelling the traces of some previous retrieve, and was about to call her back and scold her into scouring those cattails when she disappeared beneath the water.

I have since owned a Lab that swam underwater as well as an otter, but this was not something Gypsy had ever done. Yet here she was (or wasn't, for she was nowhere to be seen), diving into a pothole growing ever thick with fallen snow. Everyone in both blinds looked at me, as if to ask the same question I was asking myself—what the hell does she think she's doing?

Some anxious seconds went by, and just as I began to grow worried that she had somehow gotten mired in the thickening water, she surfaced, her back to us. Seventy yards away. And then she got her bearings, turned toward my whistle, and when she did, we saw she had a limp pintail drake in her mouth.

There have been several times in my life when I've been very proud (and some times when I've been red faced, too, but that's for another time), but I don't know if there was a much prouder moment than that. I admired her for her skill and her heart, and even for the fact that she was smart enough to ignore me and risk a possible whooping in order to get that duck. As she climbed the bank and delivered the duck to me, the men in both blinds stood up and applauded.

Gypsy was the queen of that duck camp.

It is never easy for a dog owner to watch his friend grow old, its life span so ridiculously and unfairly short. Still very much a young man, I could not fathom, as the years passed, that my girl dog was no longer also young but was nearing the end of her productive years. In fact, you might say I very much ignored the signs.

But that changed.

One very cold mid-October morning, six or seven years after the hunt just described, on the edge of an expansive prairie pothole in the middle of North Dakota, Gypsy and I, along with my brother-in-law Bill, watched the sun rise as it only can on the Great Plains. Unlike the snowy hunt, this day dawned painfully clear and cold. Ice rimmed the pothole and every cattail glistened with a hard frost.

As the sky turned from black to magenta, and as the sun crept slowly into the sky, what I didn't know was that this pothole would be the place where Gypsy would make her last retrieve. That morning, when the mallards flumped at the sound of gunfire into the ice-skimmed pothole, she entered the water with the movement of an otter, not leaping as she had always done, but slipping in slowly.

I watched nervously as the old dog broke ice for fifty yards, thrashing it to shards to fetch our birds. I'll never forget the short, whistling gasps of her breathing as she struggled. The truth came home to me, hitting me hard. Hearing those gasps, I saw in my mind the pages of years of calendars fanning rapidly by. I felt and looked no different than I had when Gypsy came into my life. But time is not so kind to dogs.

When she returned with the second bird, visibly worn, I looked deep into her eyes and saw a pain that I had never seen before: the pain of ambition that outstripped ability. I knew that she was doing what she loved most for the last time.

It is a good thing that cattails are tall. Bill could not see me. I stroked Gypsy while her head rested on my lap and her wet hips quivered with the exertion. I whispered that I loved her, thanked her for all the pleasure she had given me, and told her she was a good dog. She searched my moist eyes, hers glinting with the fire that had always been there, piercing the pain. She said to me (as plainly as if she had a voice) that she loved me and was glad, despite the pain, that she was here with me to retrieve my ducks. Oh, God, I sobbed and hugged her.

A year later Gypsy was gone. She died in early autumn, days before duck season, claimed by a cancer that ate her insides. I watched her fail for a week before I could screw up the courage to take her to the veterinarian. As I held her head on the cold steel table, crying but not caring who saw, I watched the needle slip into her vein. When she shuddered with death, she was breathing deeply through a duck wing I held before her nose.

She was my friend. She was my youth. Both are gone.

I have since been owned by two other wonderful black Labs, Rascal and Wigeon, each with his own tales of glory. But Gypsy will always be special, for she was the first and, in many ways, the best. Poised. Queenly. Devoted. And forever, a free spirit.

It is a hard, hard thing, but one must calculate this emotional expense in the cost of being a dog owner. In our lives, we may own several dogs, and just by doing so, will feel the pain of just as many final partings. That they are so faithful, so joyful, so giddily optimistic is their payment to us—a payment that only puts us further in their debt. I will have lived my life well if I am as good a man as my dogs have been dogs.

The price of a good dog? I'm not sure there is one.

But in Gypsy's case, I am absolutely certain that no one has ever spent a better five dollars and a quarter.

OLD DOGS

by Richard E. Massey

The smoke from the old briar pipe curled out and was blown straight sideways by a northern wind that shrieked down the lake. A line of men crouched and watched for ducks on Tennis Shoe Pass, north of my hometown on the prairies of western Minnesota. This pass was actually a country road diked up to cross the lake. Ducks had to pass through on their way up and down it.

Whitecaps hissed against the opposite shoreline across the highway. A line of birds raced down the lake, heading for the pass.

"Mark!" commanded my old man, setting down his pipe and crouching to his knees. All eyes were now on the ducks. It was a duck day on a Minnesota pass. The conditions were excellent for gunning. The big lake was running strong, and a migration of bluebills had just moved in with November. The pass was loaded that day—the duck hunters had moved in along with the ducks. The fall bluebill shoot was always well attended in those days.

FIVE

〰

It was then possible—indeed, if a man were good, it was probable—to bring home a limit of eighteen divers from that lake, sometimes within two hours. As the line of ducks broke over the pass, guns began to pop. I'll always remember that day for the series of events that began just after those shots.

A big chestnut-colored dog tiptoed across the edge ice that bordered the shoreline, ending forty yards out on the lake. It was an old dog I knew well, Earl Maher's Pal. Earl was my father's best friend and like a second old man to me. Pal plunged into the open water and began retrieving ducks. A snorting began that I could hear even over the howl of the wind. Earl, my dad, and I had driven to the lake in the wee hours of a bone-cold morning, and now, with luck, we could go home with three limits by noon. With luck.

The duck dog was snorting out and back, grabbing ducks, carefully laying each one on the ice shelf before swimming out for more. Time was running short for the old dog, I thought, as two dead ducks drifted away from him down the lake, blown by the wind. From their blinds along the shore, all the men could sense something was going wrong for old Pal. He had made the last two retrieves against the current and wind, and it had taken something out of him. He couldn't get up on the ice ledge. Front paws thrown over the shelf ice, he struggled for purchase. Time after time we watched him heave himself up onto the ice, but each time he sank back into the gun-blue water. We all strained with him, muscles tightening. A flock of five ducks sneaked through the pass, but no one was watching. All of us watched the dog. He was hanging there now.

"He'll get his breath and go," yelled my old man to Earl. It seemed as though he might be right. As Pal clung to the ice, I could see his flanks heaving in and out. His plume of frosty breath cooled and whitened his muzzle. One duck in the pile next to him began to kick, its leg slapping the ice, sounding like a baseball card when the spokes of a bicycle hit it. That's what it sounded like to me, anyway. I was that close to childhood.

Men had gathered on the shore with us, across the ice from Pal now, and we slowly began to realize that my old man had not guessed right. Pal was not gathering strength for another spring. Pal was done for. Pal was barely hanging on. He was shaking and shivering. The energy in his old body had been spent retrieving those ducks. He was cold. Cold and old and alone. He was whining, a sound alien to the throat of a proud dog like Pal.

I guess we never forget the day we know for sure we are grown up. I know. I can recall each incident of that whole day. I was weedy in those days, but I was tough. I was puffed up that day: I was sixteen years old, I had a best girl, and I had cracked the starting lineup of the high school football team. I was bruised from the drubbing I had received on the grid-iron the night before, but I felt good. The bluebills were in, and I was shooting the pass with the old boys, my pa's bunch.

FIVE

Not many a grown man would try to gun the pass with those old boys. It was real shooting, you see. This wasn't a deke shoot, where the ducks sail in with their legs down to land. Pass-shooting bluebills in a forty-mile-per-hour wind was the ultimate challenge in those old lead-shot days. I could gun with the best of them, and the old men who stood around me were the best. For many hunters, the science of leading a duck tearing across the pass was an unsolvable puzzle, but not to these old ballistics wizards. All of these men had put in at least fifty years with a gun in their hands. Several who stood around me now had chased Pancho Villa down in Mexico with the National Guard.

Now, as I stood with them on the shore, I could see the sorrow in each man's eyes. None of them wanted to see old Pal go under. Maybe because they were old dogs, too. These men had given me their advice and fellowship when I was little. I could recall sitting atop the shoulders or knees of all these men. I owed them all, and I owed the dog, too. He was the dog of my youth, you see. Not my dog, but the dog of my youth. His eyes sagged a little, and his broad back bowed with age. "Not much different than the old boys," I thought. Now a young heart needed to save the dog. I was needed. It was payback time.

"Get a rope!" I yelled, and those old boys snapped into action. They were like old fire horses who jumped at the clang of the bell. It didn't matter that they were almost out to pasture themselves; they rose to the occasion. I watched them moving around me as I pulled off my hippers. They were going to save that old dog whether I helped or not, I knew that. I also knew they realized the advantage my weedy young body had out there on that thin ice.

Pal was still hanging on. He had some purchase with his claws but had slid back a little into the freezing water. He would hold on until he couldn't anymore, but clearly life was slipping away. He knew his time had come. Old muscles fluttered under his oily coat. He called with a trembling voice.

I thought about what it would be like having to go to sleep that night remembering that call, and I moved. He wasn't going down that day! Yes, I knew what a cold-blooded practical man would do. A practical man would weigh the life of an old worn-down half-blind rat-tailed retriever, and he would snort. I knew that, but Pal wasn't just a bag of bones and hair. I still bear the scars on my rear where he had none too carefully clamped his jaws. I was five years old when he hit the water of Lac qui Parle Creek to save me. Earl had trained him well, and he knew when to act on his own, too. He saw me slide down the bank and into the rain-swollen current. He knew a young child shouldn't be there. His retrieve by the seat of my pants dented by dignity along with my derriere, but saved both. Now I was going to pay him back.

With a rope attached to my ankle, I began my mission. Nails had been dug out of a car trunk. With a twelvepenny in

FIVE
❧

each chopper mitt, I had two ice picks to claw my way over the ice. I moved forward with a sick feeling in my stomach. I knew the ice would be painfully thin and I'd feel a lot older by the time I reached Pal. But it was my choice, and I wanted it. Boys these days run up a high score playing Nintendo. Boys those days wanted to be outdoorsmen like their fathers.

I set my teeth and kept crawling. The ice cried under my weight and Pal cried as he saw me coming. Duck hunters know November ice. They've all stretched their luck on it a time or two. Its two-inch thickness supports, but just barely. I was down on my belly, distributing my weight. The one-inch ice ahead of me was a thin white sheet leading into some of the meanest-looking lake water I'd ever seen. My pace wasn't fast. I was snailing along on the treacherous ice. The Arctic-cold wind came tearing up the legs of my pants. Why hadn't I stuffed the cuffs into my wool socks? I stopped to pull my stocking cap down over my ears and looked back for a second at the old boys. They were flapping their arms and stomping around to keep warm there on the shore. Guns down, and ducks, flying all over the place, forgotten now.

I had to set a careful course. "I'll line up off to the side of Pal as I come across," I thought. "He's weakened the ice in front of him, that's plain. Besides, if I'm out here anyway, why not pick up the ducks? Kind of a frosting-on-the-cake routine." Did I really think it would be that easy? Yes. I'd grab the dog by the collar, let him walk back, and fetch those ducks, too.

I slid on, pushing my body with my toes now. I had given up the nails because I would need my hands free. I remember my heart nearly burst just then when an awesome sound assailed my ears: a big flock of bluebills pitched into the open water only ten feet from me. I goggled back at their beady yellow eyes. Close, at eye level, they seemed like an army of alien invaders. They had scared the liver out of me. "Yaah!" I yelled at them. The birds raced away across the surface of the water.

I looked into Pal's eyes and murmured soothingly to him. I wanted to get him ready to go. He mustn't panic and lunge, or we might both be plunged into the water.

"Let's go, old buddy," I whispered as I reached over to grab his collar. I remember thinking at the time how old he had gotten. That bluish-milky cast in his nearly blind eyes shone out at me. He turned his head to face the shore and the old boys. They were yelling encouragement. He seemed to be focused on the sound of their voices, concentrating. As I stretched slowly toward him, his eyes centered and set on me. With a groan of arthritic pain, he lunged for me. I grabbed him by the loose skin on his neck and pulled.

He was out of the water in a bound. His front legs were on my back, and he was using my head as a foothold for one hind leg. I was pushed down into the lake as the thin ice began to give way. Pal ran up and over me. As he dug for shore, my back straightened out and my chest and head bobbed back to the surface. I was soaked, and my clothes began to freeze in an instant. The moment the dog had made contact with the surface ice, however, the boys had started pulling the rope. My chin scraped across the ice as they hauled me in. I didn't have time to be scared. I was flying along across the ice so fast I passed the dog and slid into shore feet-first, like a baseball player.

Greasy fleece-lined storm coats were hastily thrown over dog and boy, and we were hustled into town to get warm. They gave me a belt of brandy, and one of them shoved a cigar into my mouth. It was a time to celebrate. We sat in the back booth of Stan Ronning's café, telling stories, staying warm, listening to the *drip, drip, drip* of my frozen clothes thawing out over the oil burner. It had been quite a day. I knew then, as I dunked my doughnut into a cup of scalding coffee, that it was a special day, one I would never forget.

Pal? He was none the worse for wear. Like the old boys, he was tasting the tough side of life. He was down, but clearly not out and, like the old boys, he still had a few good years left to shuffle around the duck sloughs.

YOUR PENDING ARRIVAL

by Doug Larsen

Memo: Karybrook's Chief William Buckshot of Black Train
From: The Office of Senior Management
Re: Your Pending Arrival

S ome years ago I took a new job out of state and was very
apprehensive about taking it. But, about a week before
the move, I got a letter from my soon-to-be new boss.
The letter welcomed me to the company, and it explained
some things about the job. It was nice of him to send it, and
it allayed a lot of the fears I had. So, as your new boss, I
thought I'd send something similar to you, and I want to take
this opportunity to welcome you to our little company and
say that we look forward to seeing you very soon. We also
look forward to calling you "Billy," rather than addressing
you via your more formal paper title. I have taken the liberty
of preparing a special identification badge for you with your

name and our address imprinted on it. Like the identification badges worn at some secure facilities and factories, it is mandatory that you wear this around your neck each day. But, unlike those worn by the folks at the secure facilities, your tag is not required so you can get in. Rather, you'll need to wear it so that we can track you down in case you get out.

I don't know if you have heard anything about our company, but ours continues to be a small, family enterprise, and I thought I might take a moment in advance of your arrival to explain your specific duties to you. I might add that many of these duties will fall outside of your practical and historical job descriptions. I regret that we did not have time to discuss these special duties in detail. Frankly, during the short interview process, there was hardly time for us to speak privately—what with the way all of the other candidates keep poking their noses in our business, interrupting, and jumping up on us as we tried to connect on a personal and professional level. The fact that two of the other candidates saw fit, rather rudely I would add, to urinate on my boot did not hurt your prospects in the least. And yes, it was easy for them to chase the pigeon wing on a string after they had seen you do it, but by then I had my mind made up that you were the man for the job. By the way, in the modern workplace, you would be fined, sued, or worse if you disclosed that you are looking for an applicant of a specific gender, so let's keep this between us, but the company's managers had their hearts set on a male employee even before the selection process began.

First, here is the lay of the land with regard to the higher-ups in our company. There are two members of Senior Management: I am one and the other is my closest associate, the Company Facilitator. I can tell you that, based on my long experience with our day-to-day operations, the Facilitator's title is one that is quite well deserved, and you should know that she rules with a tungsten hand—which, as you may have seen advertised, hits even harder than steel. She is in charge of a variety of company functions, ranging from custodial services to transportation, accounting, entertainment, and, last, laundry, which is her least favorite. The Facilitator is directly responsible for the junior executives in the firm, and consequently she works extremely long hours. She is also in charge of our cafeteria, which is centrally located on the first floor and is the hub of our facility.

Now, to the junior executives, of which there are three. While none of them have enjoyed a long tenure with us, the Facilitator and I are very, very dedicated to their advancement, and that remains a core goal here at the company, despite the fact that they have only twelve, five, and three years of experience with us, respectively. While you will be working with the junior executives, most of your daily interaction with them will be during informal meetings and outings, including the company's Reconnaissance, Orientation, and Managerial Participation outings or ROMPS.

SIX

༄

As for me personally, while I oversee and participate in many of the same tasks as the Facilitator, I am also directly responsible for procurement, as well as for landscaping and general maintenance, including the motor pool. I will also direct recreational activities for you and for the junior executives, and I will be in charge of your training program, so you will report to me daily. I do pledge that I will make your work environment as pleasant and productive as possible, and I have recently acquired a wide variety of new and interesting training tools for our work sessions from one of our favorite corporate partners in Nebraska, Cabela's Industries. While I look forward to putting many of them to good use, in both dry and aquatic scenarios—I would ask that you not mention these recent acquisitions to the Facilitator. She is not directly involved with the accounting department, and from time to time I receive, shall we say, unauthorized shipments of equipment and supplies that are stored in the garage with the motor pool. These shipments are eased quietly and gradually into the company system.

While I am usually off premises in my procurement capacity for a large portion of the day, our time together will be frequent. We will endeavor to meet daily in the late afternoon and early evening. You will find that I am typically very enthusiastic about our time together, and I expect that you will find my enthusiasm infectious. I am particularly looking forward to a number of business trips we'll be taking together in the third and fourth quarters—these promise to be ideal opportunities for you to shine in your new position.

Meanwhile, while I'm away, you will be on call every day, and as you become more and more familiar with our facility, you will be expected to take over as acting Chief of Security, and serve as First Alert Assistant in case of smoke or fire. You will be shown a feature-length training video titled *Lady and the Tramp* by the junior executives sometime during your first week. Of course, you'll live on the company premises full-time, so a bit about accommodations then.

You will have your own private accommodation, which has been ergonomically created for you by a Maine-based designer, Mr. L. L. Bean. You will be located on the second level in the Senior Management wing, in the corner. Please note that the Facilitator and I are lodged in the same quarters on that level. While you are entirely welcome to share the quarters, please note that the Facilitator is (I'm speaking somewhat out of school here) touchy about sharing the same specific accommodation. She has had her accommodation designed, and at no small expense I might add, by representatives of the Furniture Gallery and an independent design consultant, Mr. Ethan Allen, and she is none too happy about sharing them, except with yours truly. However, on occasions when the Facilitator is not in residence, you are most welcome to abandon your small, round bed and join me at your discretion. I might also add that Mr. Riley, our middle executive, would greatly appreciate your company any-time during the evening hours, especially if there is any sign of unsettled weather—and especially if it involves thunder and you don't mind a good hugging. You'll find that he will always be more than willing to have you bunk with him. Mr. Riley is located just down the hall from the Facilitator and myself. You'll find his quarters at the first door on your left, across from the junior executives' washroom. The wash-room, by the way, is where you'll find one of several of our floor-mounted drinking fountains for your exclusive use. Assuming the lid is up, you may always help yourself.

As to transportation, as mentioned earlier, I head the motor pool, and I have made preparations for your comfort-able arrival. You will note that we do reserve a specific por-tion of our vehicles for you, and while you are asked to remain in the rear of the vehicles, please know that this has no bearing upon your position here—but rather it is done solely with your safety in mind. I do hope you will enjoy look-ing out the two large side windows that are provided for your viewing pleasure. They will be opened during warmer weather, and in this company it is not looked upon as being ill mannered to just stick your nose or your whole head out of either window, as you see fit. Speaking of transportation, you might make a note that Messrs. Lund and Mercury, both representatives from our Marine Transportation Department, will be along on many of our journeys together.

They generally travel in very close proximity to the management vehicle, and in season they also transport our entire inventory of supplies from the G&H and Herters companies. Note that they will always be found traveling behind us, never to either side or, heaven forbid, in front of us. Please keep an eye on both of them for me, as we travel, or if we stop for fuel or directions. You'll find that your view of them will be quite close at hand, directly out of the rear window, and your help in this regard will be greatly appreciated.

In addition to motor vehicles, the junior executives are frequently involved with the operation of many other modes of transportation. Some are rather primitive in nature, carts or wagons—even sleds. Others are just small, two- or three-wheeled contraptions. You may be asked to pull some of these vehicles on occasion, usually via some sort of crudely devised harness system that the executives have designed on an impromptu basis. I would ask you to humor the younger generation in this regard, and know that, generally speaking, your journey will be a short one—perhaps just around the company grounds or just to a meeting of other junior executives of nearby companies. You might also be asked by some of the younger folks to wear specific garments on one or more of the theme days they enjoy each year. It may be a crown, a sash in a patriotic theme for Independence Day, or a cone-shaped birthday cap, comical antlers, or even a Santa hat for the Christmas holidays. Miss

Susan, the eldest of the junior executives, enjoys entertaining, and you may be asked to attend some of her formal summer tea parties along with a small, blond woman named Barbie (nobody seems to know her last name) and others in her inner circle of companions. This may or may not require a hat on your part, but if one is needed, it will be supplied for you. Again, I'd ask you to remember that these episodes are usually short lived and are not meant to cause you any specific embarrassment, so please look upon these occasions as opportunities to bond with your coworkers, and be thankful that they are including you. Remember, these are the same folks that, owing to their opposable thumbs, can throw Frisbees and sticks. They can also turn on the sprinklers and run through them with you when it gets truly hot in the (pardon the expression) dog days of summer.

As to our cafeteria, you are welcome in the cafeteria at any time and it is truly a twenty-four-hour, seven-day-a-week facility. We offer several meals daily for the staff, and even though the fare served will smell and appear very interesting, please know that we will be arranging a private seating and specific menu for you each day. It was my experience with the beloved but frustrating staff member that held your position previously, as it has been with other workers of your background, that you may find some offerings in the cafeteria virtually irresistible. However, I would ask you to please resist the urge to attempt to "borrow" any items that are left unattended, as I can promise you that no good will come of it. I recall some years ago when your predecessor quietly absconded with a whole chicken that was defrosting in the sink. He spirited it out to a shady spot on the company lawn, where he proceeded to devour the poultry in question. The subject of the subsequent investigation refused to speak up in his own defense, and chose instead to adopt the clichéd position of someone with his tail between his legs. The Facilitator wasted no time in gathering several items of very damning evidence against the perpetrator—which included a shredded paper wrapper that had once contained giblets. The employee partner was disciplined rather sternly and was directed to sleep on the extreme lower level of our head-quarters that evening, which I am sorry to say offers just basic accommodation, and is rather cool and damp. Similar experiences have occurred with pies, portions of cakes, sticks of butter, and various pork products. Take my advice, Billy, and avoid any unauthorized contact with these cafeteria staples—as any episode of this sort will just upset the Facilitator. She will record it in your personnel file, where it will remain for two calendar years, which I would remind you is fourteen years—a lifetime—on your clock.

Calling cards: I hesitate to even discuss this messy business, but to be blunt, please leave your calling cards on company grounds, but not on the grounds of the Kelly Company, located next door. Depending on the proximity of your card to the Kellys' front entrance, leaving a card there often results in an impromptu and usually very unpleasant meeting with their president, who favors very expensive Italian shoes and has little interest in our business. Frankly, Mr. Kelly has been especially sensitive since we opened our Waterfowl-Smoking Department in an old refrigerator behind the motor pool, and in addition to the calling card problem, apparently he does not appreciate the smell of smoldering hickory chips.

As to your collection tasks, many of your early tasks will be errand running—short errands that will be easy to handle at first—and these will gradually be made longer and more difficult as your confidence in your own abilities increases. At that time, and when I deem it appropriate, you will be placed full in charge of the company's collection department. You'll be introduced to the company's short-haul delivery system, or the Launcher, which literally hurls compact packages at great speeds and also generates an immediate report. You will also answer to another department head, Mr. Acme, and while he is curt and speaks with quite a high-pitched voice, you will find that the easiest way to get along with him is by paying attention and obeying his commands to the very best of your abilities. Both will be present at all of our training sessions, which will occur four to five times per week.

Assuming that everything progresses well through the summer months, we will move to the outing schedule. Most of your collections will be made in agricultural or aquatic areas, where we will meet two to three times a week during the third and fourth quarters. We will not be the only attendees at these meetings, however; Mr. Remington will also join us. He is also in the Collections Department, and you will find he is a very forceful speaker. He has days when he is devastatingly effective, and others when your patience will surely be tried. I'll warn you that most of these meetings begin very early—as early as 4:30 A.M.—and you'll often be expected to make mental notes of the location of specific packages before you are sent to retrieve them. There will be some local collections early in the schedule, but as the third-quarter weather gets progressively worse, most of our more desirable packages will be arriving from Canada. Typically, if we are quite lucky and business is brisk, there will be several packages, or as many as six, to collect each day. Often our meetings will not be scheduled in advance. Rather, based upon my experience, if I expect a delivery from Canada, I will advise the Facilitator on the evening prior to our meeting, she will sign off on our request, and we will depart very early and very quietly. I think you will enjoy these meetings immensely.

Finally, while both the Facilitator and myself will endeavor to keep our relationship with you as professional as possible, I must honestly tell you that, practically, it is quite difficult to do so, living in such close proximity. Thus, please excuse my frequent pats on the back, scratches behind the ears, or rubs on the belly. While the Facilitator displays a cool exterior, as she did with our last employee partner, you'll find that she will be the first person by your side in a time of need, whether it be a little thing like a cut pad—or a huge crisis such as a confrontational meeting with a skunk. When several months ago your predecessor left to make your position available, the Facilitator displayed a great deal of emotion, since the white-whiskered Jack had been a loyal and faithful employee for eleven wonderful years. Even now, I am too moved to share details with you, but Jack had a good life, and one day his old heart just played out. It was certainly a better end than many have had at the hands of screeching brakes or poison or disease, so I guess we should feel blessed. I cried like a baby at his passing, and I am just as emotional about having you join us. New beginnings are just that, and in you we see great promise and potential just begging to be harnessed. So, welcome! We look forward to having you with us, and the junior executives have an old tennis ball they would like to share with you as soon as you arrive.

BOLOGNA HUNTERS

by Wade Bourne

T he South Dakota prairie rolled toward the sunset like waves of a still, quiet sea. The landscape was broken only by occasional trees and fences and gullies. Every mile or so a farmstead stood surrounded by thick hedges that were planted to fend off winter's wind. In surrounding fields, stubble was all that remained of corn and milo crops that had stood tall just a few weeks ago.

We'd finally made it to pheasant country! My two partners and I had talked about this trip for years. We'd always wanted to try hunting ringnecks. Now we planned to head out the next morning, knocking on farmers' doors and asking permission to sample the bounty of these broad plains.

Don Buck, Philip Sumner, and I have been close friends since childhood, and we've shared a mutual passion for waterfowl hunting. We've collaborated on many adventures, including several trips to Canada to chase ducks and geese before the season opened back home in Tennessee. We had the art of the road trip down pat: pile our gear in the back of Don's Blazer, spread an old Army blanket for the dogs, then drive to whatever destination we'd picked—gas, fast food, and pit stops only.

But this year we were going after other game. Every time we'd passed through the Dakotas, we'd talked about doing a pheasant hunt some year. None of us had ever shot these gaudy birds, but we'd read about them and talked to other hunters who had. We knew we'd enjoy their challenge and the fun of trying something different.

Before heading north, we'd drawn up a game plan. A friend from South Dakota had told me that most pheasant hunting in this state takes place during the first two weeks of the season. Relatives and friends come in from all over the country, and big neighborhood hunts are the rule. Brigades of hunters line up and march across grainfields toward other lines of "blockers." Pheasants run ahead of the pushers and then flush when they realize they're trapped. In late October in South Dakota, thousands of cockbirds are bagged on these family-and-friends hunts.

Then, by early November, the big hunts are over. Waitresses in little country cafés get a breather. Dusty section roads settle out, and farmers start hunkering down for winter. Also, the pheasants that have lived through this annual trial-by-fire have Ph.D.s in hunter avoidance. When men or dogs approach, they burrow into thick cover, or they flush out of range and fly hell-bent for the next county.

Thus, the frustration of hunting these educated birds causes most locals to abandon the fields by November, which leaves them open to hunters from Tennessee who don't know any better than to go after these late-season survivors. My buddy had told me we'd find plenty land to hunt on in November, and if we'd bust enough cover with our dogs, we'd get some shooting. Not easy shooting, but perhaps enough to take a limit of roosters.

So this was our plan. We'd test it the next morning.

Our dogs were a big question mark. We had two Labrador retrievers, my yellow male, named Luther, and Philip's black one-year-old, Lightning. They were "meat dogs." They had come from local litters and hadn't taken lessons from professional trainers. We'd played fetch with them since they were pups, and had taught them to sit and stay and mark falls. But mainly they were noses and legs and speed for retrieving ducks we knocked down. If they found the birds and brought them back, that's all we asked. We had no clue how they'd react when they struck the hot, quick trail of a pheasant.

But we soon learned how the next day, which will be forever etched in our ledger of fond memories.

The morning was crisp and sunny. Following my friend's advice, we drove an hour south of Pierre, where we were staying, and then stopped and asked permission to hunt a sprawling farm that had several brushy draws dividing its

SEVEN

∽

harvested milo fields. "There are still a few pheasants around," the owner told us at his doorstep. "They're wild as all get-out, but if you want to try 'em, go ahead."

We started at a nearby gully that was choked with weeds and bushy plum trees. It ran some 150 yards from the base of a stock pond dam to a farm road. Don left the truck and circled to the upwind end of the gully to block. When he was in position, Philip and I turned the dogs out, loaded our shotguns, and started working up the gully. Both Labs disappeared in the cover.

Action came almost immediately. "Hen!" Philip yelled as a brown, pointed-tail bird rocketed out of the weeds. I'd heard the pheasant fly and instinctively started to mount my shotgun, but I'd stopped myself before Philip called out. Another hen flushed thirty yards up the gully, then another. Philip and I walked fast to stay up with the dogs, which were pushing quickly toward Don.

Suddenly a fourth bird flushed, and this one had the distinctive bright markings of a rooster. I swung on him and fired. The bird plummeted in a burst of feathers. Luther appeared out of the weeds, made a beeline for the pheasant, and fetched him to me as if he'd been doing it for years.

I admired this bird only briefly, then stuffed him in my game vest and hurried to catch up with Philip. We were closing on Don's position now, and other pheasants were fleeing the cover. Some ran out the side of the gully into the stubble, but one rooster flushed right in Don's face, and he made a clean kill. Then Philip downed a rooster that flew out on his side. When the pandemonium ended, we had a trio of beautiful cock pheasants, and we also had the giddy assurance that our plan was going to work. Our dogs had done a super job of pushing birds out of the thick cover.

In the next few hours we knocked on other doors to ask permission, which was usually granted by hospitable farmers or wives who unfailingly commented on our southern accents. We hunted several more gullies and small thickets. We bagged another rooster here, another there, and by early afternoon we had our combined limit of nine. Our first day in South Dakota had been a raving success, and we had four more days to build on it.

That night we were celebrating in the bar at the Holiday Haus motel in Pierre. Customers were scarce and the bar was quiet. Don, Phillip, and I had a table along a wall. We were watching a football game and recounting the day's events.

"Where are you guys from?" asked a female voice from another table.

"Tennessee," I responded. "What about you?"

"We're from Minneapolis," the attractive, casually dressed woman answered. She was sitting with four men who were older than she was. "You go hunting today?" she continued.

"Yeah. We hunted south of Presho. We had a good day. Got our birds by midafternoon." I tried to sound like shooting a limit of pheasants was no big deal. "You all go out?"

"Yeah, we hit some fields east of town," the woman answered. "We found a few birds, but nothing spectacular. We're trying to decide where to go tomorrow.

"Can we buy a round?" she asked.

Soon we were sitting together and introductions were made. The woman was a professional dog trainer and the men were her clients. She had brought them to South Dakota to hunt and get a firsthand look at the progress their dogs had made. She didn't say so, but after a slow first day, she was feeling pressure to get her hunters into more action.

"We found several places to hunt this morning and they all had birds," I continued. "Why don't you follow us down to Presho in the morning, and maybe we can steer you toward a good area."

"That would be wonderful," the trainer beamed, "or we could join forces and hunt together. Would that be imposing on you?" she asked hopefully.

"Oh, no," I assured her. "That would be fine. We'd enjoy the company. We could meet in the restaurant for breakfast, then caravan down and start hunting by 10." I looked to Don and Philip for concurrence with this decision. They both gave me icy, I-can't-believe-you've-done-this expressions.

"Wonderful!" the trainer said. "See you around 8? By the way, we usually take a tailgate lunch. Will you eat in the field or go find a café?"

"We'll pick up something for sandwiches and eat with you," I responded. "That way we won't lose much hunting time. See you then."

The next morning, we were struck by our new companions' attire. They looked like they'd stepped out of an Orvis catalog. They were decked out in new brush pants, houndstooth-check wool shirts, and expensive boots. Their headgear consisted of tweed fedoras and suede British driving caps.

In contrast, our brier pants were faded and frayed from years of use. We wore hooded jerseys, scuffed boots, and freebie ball caps from a feed store back home.

After breakfast, we rendezvoused in the parking lot. Don pulled his Blazer up next to the trainer's late-model pickup with custom topper. Hooked behind the trainer's truck was an aluminum dog trailer with four compartments on each side.

One of the Minnesota hunters loaded into the pickup with the trainer. The other three boarded a new rental SUV.

"We need some gas and something for lunch," I called back to them as Philip and I climbed in with Don. The trainer waved, and our caravan pulled out of the Holiday Haus parking lot and crossed the street to a convenience store. While Don was pumping gas, Philip and I went inside for groceries.

"What do we need?" I asked.

"Get a couple of packs of bologna and a loaf of bread and a bottle of hot sauce," Philip answered. "I'll pick up some Cokes."

With these items stashed in Don's cooler, we set out for Presho. Once again the morning was bright. As the miles passed, Don, Philip, and I relived the joys of the previous day and speculated on what this new hunt would bring. We saw no need to change anything. We'd continue to focus on the ditches and thickets. With more hunters and dog power, we could tackle some bigger blocks of cover, but the strategy would remain the same.

We decided to start at the "six-two" farm we'd hunted the previous day (six crossroads west of the highway and two crossroads south). It had a large weed-choked draw that we'd tried to push, but couldn't cover adequately. Dozens of pheasants ran or flew away before we could get in range. This morning, however, those birds would be in for a surprise.

Don pulled his Blazer off the road next to the draw, and the two vehicles behind us did likewise. Everybody climbed out. "Lots of pheasants here yesterday," I announced to our new partners. "I think we can push this draw and jump several roosters."

At first there was no response from the Minnesota party. They surveyed the scene and shared a few inaudible comments among themselves. Then the trainer addressed us, "Don't you think it might be better to hit the milo fields?

Most birds should be out feeding this morning instead of in the cover."

Pheasants had been thick in this draw yesterday, but we hadn't hunted it until early afternoon. And what did we know about pheasant hunting anyway? We had a grand total of one day's experience—although it had been a very good day. Our new friends obviously were pheasant veterans. Perhaps their idea was better.

"OK," I acceded. "That sounds good. Where do you think we should start?"

"Let's form a line over in that field and work toward the far fencerow," she suggested.

The milo field was wide open and stretched for at least a quarter section. "It's pretty big. Do you think we can cover it?" I asked.

"Our dogs will cover it for us," the trainer answered. "We can send three blockers down to the far end of the field, then the rest of us can take the dogs and push toward them. We ought to get some shooting."

Whatever.

Don opened the hatch on his Blazer, and our two Labs popped out like corks from a champagne bottle. They were fired up. They began scratching dirt and marking tires on every vehicle. When Luther got to the dog trailer, hair rose between his shoulder blades.

"Nice looking Labs," one of the Minnesotans said. "Who trained them for you?"

"We trained them ourselves," I answered. "We mostly hunt ducks with them. This is the first time they've hunted pheasants."

"Oh," the man responded.

Don, Philip, and I started pulling on game vests and retrieving shotguns from their cases. The Minnesota hunters did likewise, and they also donned leather shooting gloves and yellow glasses.

"Look at that," Philip whispered so only Don and I could hear. One of our new friends was wiping an oily rag over a fancy Italian over-under. Its gold engraving gleamed in the morning sun. "Man, wonder what that cost?" Philip quietly asked.

All the other Minnesotans had over-unders with names that ended in "i" or "a." My shotgun was a Browning B-80 with tape around the stock, and both Don and Philip were toting Remingtons. "Boys, looks like we're hunting with the upper crust," I observed.

Soon we were ready to begin the drive. The trainer went to open one of the doors on the trailer. "Leash your dogs," she ordered us matter-of-factly.

I knew that look in Philip's eyes. Hair was probably standing up between his shoulder blades, if he had any there.

"Aw, let him out. Maybe we'll have a good old country dogfight," I joked, hoping to head off a more acerbic comment by my partner.

"Please," she insisted. "This dog is aggressive around other males, and he's too valuable to risk getting injured in a fight. Won't you hold your dogs while I turn him out?"

Philip and I grabbed our Labs' collars and held on as they strained to pull free.

When the trainer opened the door, a Brittany spaniel bounced out, and he made a beeline for Luther. High ears and tails prevailed (what little tail the Brittany had!) and suddenly the two dogs were scotched nose to nose.

"Control your dog!" I demanded. As the trainer snapped a lead on the Brittany's collar, I glanced at Philip and winked. He choked back a laugh and looked away.

Soon another Brittany—a female—was released from the trailer. Don and two of the Minnesota hunters drove the SUV around to the far end of the field and took up blocking stations. I had Luther reined down and walking at heel, but I still kept a tight grip on his collar.

"Form the line," the trainer commanded like a drill instructor in basic training.

We spread some fifty yards apart across the nearside of the field. When everyone was ready, the Minnesotans released their dogs, and Philip and I did likewise. Luther and Lightning blazed off like greyhounds. The two Brittanys loped out about twenty yards, then they began coursing back and forth parallel to the line like robots. When the trainer wanted them to reverse course, she'd yell, "Hup," and the dogs would do a 180 and run the opposite direction. Impressive!

Meanwhile, our dogs were halfway across the field toward the blockers. With no thickets or brush to hunt out, they were just covering ground. As we began advancing, Luther chased up a cock, and we watched as the bird flew into the brushy draw. "There goes one!" I yelled encouragingly.

"Can you call your dog in?" the trainer questioned.

"Luther, Luther!" I yelled. "Get in here. Heeeaal!"

"Hup!" Philip called. I looked his direction and he grinned.

And so we advanced across the milo field, five hunters in line, the two Brittanys working beautifully while our two Labs were running uncontrolled and chasing up pheasants far out of range. I felt like crawling into the next badger hole I came to.

Suddenly Luther jumped a jackrabbit, and a torrid chase was on! Neither animal could gain ground on the other. Luther yipped a series of high-pitched barks as he tore after his quarry—out the side of the field, through the bordering draw, and over a low ridge several hundred yards distant. As they crossed the rise, I could see a small brown dot followed at short distance by a bigger yellow dot, boring across the prairie. I didn't know if I'd ever see Luther again.

"He certainly has good speed," one of the Minnesota hunters commented. I felt like poking him!

We continued pushing across the field with Lightning and the two Brittanys working the stubble. Pheasants were flying and running out the sides. As we drew near the blockers, several hens flushed, but roosters were scarce. Finally one of the Brittanys flushed a rooster that sailed right over Don's head. He tracked and fired three times, and the bird flew on untouched. We ended this first drive scoreless.

As we waited for the vehicles to be brought up, Luther came trotting back, panting hard and tongue wagging. He wouldn't make eye contact with me, like a teenager caught tasting forbidden fruit.

We moved to another field and set up a second drive. Again, we saw several pheasants, but most flushed or ran out of range. One of the Minnesota hunters made a nice shot on a rooster that took wing as our trap closed, and Philip crippled a bird that flushed at marginal distance. Lightning raced after it, caught it, and brought it back. At least there was one ray of sun among our figurative showers.

"Why don't we break for lunch," the trainer suggested. "We'll give the dogs a rest and decide what to try this afternoon."

Conversation among our group was limited as we gathered back at the vehicles. Don, Philip, and I left our Labs out and poured them some water. The trainer put her two

Brittanys—a different pair from the first drive—back in the trailer. Then she unlocked her truck and retrieved two large picnic baskets and a cooler. She opened the baskets, spread a plaid tablecloth over the tailgate, and began arranging a banquet.

She laid out delicious-looking roast beef sandwiches, wrapped in plastic. She also had potato salad, summer sausage, smoked salmon, club crackers, a small round of cheese, pickles, olives, a bag of bananas and apples, brownies, and oatmeal cookies. For beverages she had hot coffee, spring water, and a bottle of chardonnay! The Minnesota hunters served from this buffet onto Melmac plates. They ate with plated flatwear, drank from real glasses, and wiped their mouths on cloth napkins.

We had bologna, loaf bread, hot sauce, and canned sodas. We didn't even have paper towels. We took our meager fixings and eased behind Don's Blazer to slap sandwiches together and commiserate about how the morning had gone.

"I say, old boy, how's the bologna?" I chided Philip. When he raised his sandwich for a bite, hot sauce squished out and ran down his hand.

"I'm not amused," he answered acerbically. "I don't think I've ever been so embarrassed in my life."

Don joined in: "They must think we're the biggest hicks that ever came out of the hills. We probably ought to be traveling in a pickup with a rocking chair in the back. The Clampetts do South Dakota." We all chuckled.

"I'll tell you what we are," Philip interjected, eyeing his sandwich. "We're bologna hunters. They're tenderloin-and-wine hunters, and we're bologna hunters. We're untrained dogs and rusty shotguns."

"Yeah, well, I'll tell you what. This bologna hunter's had enough of this co-op business," I chimed in. "We were into pheasants yesterday, and we haven't shot squat this morning. I'm sorry I got us into this mess, and I know how to get us out of it."

"What are you going to do?" Philip asked.

"I'm going to lay down a little Tennessee law," I replied.

They both broke into big grins. "Here comes de judge," Don guffawed, and he toasted me with his Coke can.

The Minnesota hunters had finished their meal, and the trainer was repacking the picnic baskets. "Could I have a word with you?" I asked.

"Sure. What's up?" she replied.

"I think we're going off on our own this afternoon," I continued. "This idea of hunting together isn't working. Our dogs aren't trained to hunt the fields, and it's obvious we're holding you back. We had good shooting yesterday hitting the little cover patches. I think we'd be better off getting back to that, and you-all can go hunt however you want."

She looked at me for a few seconds without saying anything. Then she responded, "Tell you what. Why don't we stick together for another drive or two, and we'll try the cover. Our way didn't work this morning, so let's try yours this afternoon. We'll push some of the bigger ditches, and if we still don't have any luck, then we'll split up."

"Sounds like a deal," I answered, and I went back to Philip and Don to share this plan.

We decided to try the big draw we'd passed on earlier. This time Don and three of the Minnesota hunters circled around to block. When they were in position, the rest of us plowed into the cover. Philip and I were on the left with our Labs, and the trainer and one of her clients covered the right with two Brittanys.

Our dogs got birdy as soon as we started pushing. Luther and Lightning disappeared into a stand of cattails that bordered the ditch in the middle of the draw. The Brittanys were working close up the right slope.

Suddenly pheasants started erupting from the reeds. "Hen! Hen! Hen!" Philip called as individual birds took wing. "Rooster!"

This pheasant angled up the right side of the draw, and the Minnesota hunter made a clean one-shot kill. One of the Brittanys bounced out and fetched the bird back to its trainer.

Twenty yards later Luther flushed another rooster from the cattails, and Philip busted him. Luther marked the fall perfectly, raced in, and retrieved the pheasant like a pro.

Action got better as we closed the distance to the blockers. Now hens were flushing one after another. Two cockbirds flushed at the edge of the draw and sailed out over the milo. Another cock flew up in front of Don and he dropped him. One of the Minnesota hunters did likewise to another bird. When the action finally ceased, we'd taken six roosters and missed two more, a vast improvement over the morning. "Where can we find another cover patch like this?" the trainer asked with a smile.

The next three hours were some of the most enjoyable I've ever spent afield. We pushed several gullies and thickets, and found pheasants in each one. Also, hunting the cover was a more efficient use of our man- and dog-power. We could surround some of the smaller spots, trapping the birds before turning our dogs in to chase them up. Then, when a rooster flushed, somebody was going to get a shot.

By late afternoon we'd bagged nineteen roosters, with five to go for a party limit. Our Labs had held their own against the Minnesota Brittanys. They'd put up more than half the birds we'd taken. It was fun to watch them on the trail of a pheasant running through the cover. Both dogs would get an ears-up, tail-high look, and then they'd spring through the brush in hot pursuit until the bird flushed.

We had time for one more drive before sunset. We decided to hunt through a deep ravine between two milo fields. We'd gotten permission to hunt this farm the day before, but we'd bypassed the gulch because of its size. Now, though, we could cover it efficiently.

We used the same strategy as earlier: four blockers, four pushers, and four dogs. When everyone was in place, Philip called, "Let's go," and we started marching forward.

We hadn't gone thirty yards when Luther jumped another jackrabbit. He bolted when he saw the rabbit run. "Luther!" I yelled forcefully. The Lab stopped in his tracks, looked back at me sheepishly, then turned to watch the rabbit bound up the side of the ravine. When the jack had disappeared, Luther trotted back into the cover and continued hunting pheasants.

The trainer was forty yards to my left. "Nice job," she called. "He's a quick learner." I swelled with pride.

Once again birds started boiling out of the ravine—mostly hens. The roosters were sticking tight or running ahead of the dogs. Every so often we'd catch a glimpse of one darting through an opening in the grass. He'd be stretched out low to the ground and going like a roadrunner.

Suddenly a rooster flushed right in my face, a rush of flapping and cackling and color! He nearly took my cap off as he flew over my head and sped away. I quickly regained my composure, spun around, shouldered my Browning, and fired. The bird fell in an explosion of feathers. Luther bounded in for the retrieve.

One of the Minnesota blockers scored next, then Don made a beautiful crossing shot on a rooster at forty yards. "Great shot!" I called. "Be careful, now. We only need two more."

I'd hardly spoken the words when a pair of roosters flushed together in front of Philip. He'd grown up a quail hunter; his reaction was classic. He smoothly mounted his shotgun, fired, and maxed the first bird. Then he switched off to the second and centered it in his pattern. As the birds fell, our two dogs bounded in to fetch them, Lightning picking up one and Luther the other. They acted like they'd hunted pheasants all their lives.

"That's it. No more," the trainer called ahead to the blockers. As we began unloading our shotguns, she looked my way and graciously said, "Thanks for including us today. This was a super hunt." I smiled and nodded back.

∾

The drive back to Pierre seemed shorter than sixty miles. Don, Philip, and I were almost giddy at how the day had gone. We'd started low, but we'd finished high. The bologna boys had come through! So, too, had the bologna dogs! We relived each bird. We laughed about Luther's jackrabbit chase. Philip and I kidded Don about missing that first bird. We also talked about the spread our Minnesota partners had enjoyed at lunch, and we chuckled about our own sparse menu.

The headlights of the trainer's truck were close behind. We were all meeting for dinner back at the hotel. "Perhaps I'll order chateaubriand or Peking duck," I noted impertinently.

"Know what I'm ordering?" Philip asked. "I'm ordering a bologna steak, fried in bacon grease. I'm going to send a note to the chef to slice it as thick as a nickel is wide, then to sear it quickly on both sides and leave it pink in the middle."

"Excellent choice, my good man," I responded. "And what wine will you order with your meal?"

"The cheapest in the house!" he answered as the lights of Pierre appeared over the next rise.

8

HUNTER'S MOON

by Chuck Petrie

Every year, on the Hunter's Moon, they come. You won't know they've arrived by watching the skies. You'll just find them one morning on a bog lake. Maybe a few dozen ringnecks at first. A few days later, perhaps fifty or a hundred more. But that's all. All the small dark-water lake will accommodate.

There must be a relationship between the birds that appear here one year and those that arrived the year before and the year before that. Northern Wisconsin has many bog lakes in its arboreal latitudes, but the ringnecks return each year to only a few, as if these stopping places are taught by one generation of ducks to the next.

By mid-October the North's wild rice lakes are nearly void of the mallards and black ducks that migrate southward with the first frosts and threatening northerlies. Bluebills have yet to arrive on the big lakes and flowages, so waterfowl hunting comes to a temporary standstill, and hunters turn to ruffed grouse covers when the weather moderates to bluebird days of Indian summer.

On these warm, sunny days, if you're lucky you'll find partridge. If you're even luckier, you may discover one of the backwoods lakes rimmed with purple leatherleaf, Labrador tea, and highbush cranberry, and, surrounding this low, spongy, floating mat of vegetation, emerald green spruce and smoky gold tamaracks. Approach the water and you may see it flecked with distinct patterns of black and white—ringnecks languidly paddling on the surface. If you're lucky.

Stay hidden in the spruce and tamarack fringe and watch. The birds dive and resurface, dive and resurface, feeding on the tiny protein-rich invertebrates that flourish, for some reason, in this bog lake but not in the ten or twenty others in a five-mile radius.

You've found a ringneck lake, a prize the northern wing-shooter covets and the location of which he will share with few others, only the trusted few with whom he hunts his favorite woodcock or grouse covers. That's how Gunnar, my chocolate Lab, and I found our ringneck lake—while grouse hunting—three years ago. In fact, a grouse led us to it. The bird flushed wild, but we saw it and followed. Looking ahead, through the oak and aspen, anticipating a reflush, I suddenly noticed a green background—spruce trees. Through the dense limbs of the firs, a hint of sunlight sparkled on the water.

Gunnar quartered ahead, still searching, for what he wasn't sure. It was his puppy year. Barely five months old, he couldn't clear most deadfalls. He'd hurdle a downed tree but not all of his body found its way over the top. He'd hang up, his hindquarters dangling over the downed tree, a backward glance of "Help me, Dad," in his innocent vibrant puppy eyes.

We descended the shallow bowl enclosing the lake and pushed through the thick firs to the boggy perimeter. Only ten acres of water, but massed on the other side of the lake, in the reflection of tamarack and spruce ringing the shore, were more than a hundred ringnecks.

I retreated to the spruce fringe and watched the ducks for half an hour. Gunnar didn't even see them. His puppy-world comprehension was still limited to the irresistible objects he could reach in a few helter-skelter bounds. The ducks, to him, might just have well been in the next county. If I dropped a bird in the water, the dog would neither see it nor retrieve it. We hunted our way back to the pickup, hoping to find another grouse, then drove three miles on the old logging road to the county highway and headed home.

We returned to the lake twice more in the next week. The ducks were there. On our third visit a few days later, they were gone.

ॐ

The following October, Gunnar was ready. We checked the lake early in the month but found no ducks. A day after the full moon, the Hunter's Moon, we returned. Sixty or seventy ringnecks were loafing on the water when we sneaked through the trees.

I slid two three-inch No. 2 steel loads into my over-under and walked out of the tree cover toward the lake, Gunnar at heel. As soon as they saw us, the ducks began paddling toward the opposite shore, and then took off. I kneeled down in the sphagnum moss underlying the thick, waxy-leafed leatherleaf and waited, knowing what would happen. The ducks would have to circle, their small wings beating furiously, to gain the altitude necessary to clear the treetops. I'd seen it on other small lakes like this one—from where they had flushed, the ringnecks would need to complete at least a half circle around the lake. As they did, they'd come over me, offering a shot. Had they been mallards or any other ducks, I'd have stayed hidden and not shot on the flush; instead, I'd sit and wait for the birds to trickle back in small groups or as singles and doubles. Ringnecks will dribble back the same way, but, unlike other ducks, one or two parting shots won't keep them from returning to their roost.

The birds were coming, gaining altitude quickly. I rose and started swinging as they came over me. Concentrating on a drake near the rear of the flock, I pulled on the bird and fired, folding it, but couldn't get off another shot. The rest of the ducks were already over the trees.

The drake's momentum carried it over the shore, where it plummeted into knee-deep brush beyond a clump of stunted spruce. Gunnar had a bead on the falling bird and bounded after it as soon as he heard my "Back" command. His mark on the downed duck was better than mine, and in a few seconds he picked it out of the thick moss and bog plants and delivered it to hand.

I slid the ringneck into my game pocket and looked for some cover. There was no wind. I knew the birds would circle the bog as they came back to roost, checking for danger, offering me a shot in the process. How ironic, I thought, that their vigilance would be their undoing. But these ducks had probably never heard shooting or seen a human before. They'd be looking, perhaps, for movement betraying a bobcat or coyote or mink on shore, or a hawk or eagle perched on top of a tree near the lake. There was no way they'd know their careful scouting flight would bring them, again, over the two most dangerous predators on the lake that day.

Gunnar and I hid between two highbush cranberry shrubs and watched the sky. The ducks' return would be like their departure: They'd come in fast, and once they dipped below the dark circle of firs, they'd be hard to see. It would be quick overheads or crossing shots over the water. I popped the empty case from my shotgun and slid in a fresh round.

A shrill sound like tearing silk was my first clue that birds were returning. A group of four suddenly appeared from behind us and flashed overhead, wings locked in an air-splitting power dive. Before I could shoot, they were out of range, lighting on the far side of the lake. Having reached the water, the ducks immediately started to preen, uncon-cerned now that they'd safely returned. As I watched them, I saw movement to my left as a single came down low and fast, crossing to my right. Two quick shots sprayed water far behind the hen. She never missed a wingbeat, just kept going on her predetermined course to join the small flock across the water. Five minutes later, two missed shots at a pair coming from the other direction…and a baleful stare from a Labrador retriever.

A longer wait and redemption. A lone drake coming head-on. My second shot broke a wing as he flared directly above me. The duck collapsed, dropping only twenty feet away near a clump of leafless brush adorned with bright red rose hips. Another dry retrieve for Gunnar.

Two ducks were enough for that day. With the misses and the two birds dropped, I'd done enough shooting. Even ringnecks will only tolerate so much. We stayed, though, pondering the bog plants, now quiescent with the coming of winter—and watched the ringnecks slowly return. When there was still an hour of shooting light left, most had come back to the water. Watching them streak down over the lake, sometimes in twos or threes or fours like flights of jet fight-ers in precise wing-to-wing formation, skidding to a landing on the quiet water, was pleasure enough.

Three days later we returned again. This time we had company. Dave had come north from southern Wisconsin for several days of grouse hunting and muskie fishing. October is the month of big muskies in Wisconsin, but Dave and my brother Tom decided to forgo fishing for an afternoon of ringneck hunting.

Walking single file through decaying oak and aspen leaves, the musty-sweet fragrance of autumn permeating the grouse woods, we were glad to be isolated, out of view of other hunters. The strange assembly of gear we carried was a dead giveaway of the plan we'd concocted. It was one of those collective brainstorms hunting buddies occasionally think of that, if it works, will be replayed around campfires for years. If not, no one will ever mention it again.

Slipping through the barrier of trees surrounding the lake, we saw more ringnecks on the lake than I'd ever seen before. Almost two hundred birds took off from the water as we hurried toward the boggy shore. We had agreed not to shoot as the ducks departed—an extra precaution, part of our plan.

Tom put down the bag he was carrying and pulled two bluebill decoys from it. "Close enough. Ringnecks aren't that particular," he said, tying the first decoy to the end of the thiry-pound-test braided line on Dave's muskie rod.

"Give me about three feet of slack, Dave."

Dave hit the free-spool button on the big casting reel, releasing the required line.

Tom tied on the second bluebill and then deferred to Dave, "Have at her. They weigh more than the biggest muskie plug, but a slow heave should get them out there without breaking the rod."

Dave stepped cautiously toward the water, testing each step on the springy border of bog foliage.

"Careful," I warned. "You're standing over ten feet of water. If you break through that thin layer of vegetation, you'll float your hat."

He took one more calculated step and eased the rod back over his shoulder, the two decoys swaying pendulously from the tip of the heavy pole. Using a two-handed swing, he heaved the blocks over his head, toward the water. The decoys clumsily arced skyward, then dropped quickly and landed with a SPLAT! thirty feet from shore.

"That should do it." Dave assured us. "With the wind at our back, they should stay put."

We looked at the decoys floating on the lake, at the muskie rod, now lying partly concealed on the sphagnum moss, and at each other, chuckling inwardly.

"We're going to feel pretty stupid if this turns into a rhubarb," Dave warned.

"That's OK," Tom reassured us. "No one will know but us. And if it doesn't work, I know at least I'm not going to be talking about it. Let's spread out a little and get ready."

Gunnar and I settled down between two six-foot-tall tamaracks and waited for the story to unfold. I looked to my right, at Dave, huddled behind a short spruce, and Tom, beyond him, squatting behind a cranberry bush. We were ready.

"Coming in at nine o'clock," Tom alerted us. "A single."

The bird came fast, and even though it didn't appear ready to land, it headed straight for the decoys.

Tom's 12-gauge shattered the quiet as his shot rolled the bird in midair, dropping it twelve feet outside the decoys.

"Nice shot," Dave congratulated Tom.

"Get down," I warned. "Here come two more."

Again, the birds headed straight for the decoys, but this pair started wing-rocking, putting their brakes on to land with the blocks. Dave and I stood and fired simultaneously, knocking the lead bird down. It hit the water at a low angle, skipping twice across the surface before coming to rest.

I took Gunnar away from the lay of the fishing line so he wouldn't have to swim over it, and, still twenty feet from water's edge, gave him a line on the first bird. "Back!" I commanded, realizing this would be his first water retrieve on our little ringneck lake.

Gunnar took off like a wheel-smoking dragster. Ten feet from the water, though, where the floating mat of bog vegetation grew thin, he suddenly looked like a drunk crossing an underinflated waterbed. Then he stiff-legged to a halt and stood bobbing up and down on the springy mat of vegetation, staring intently at the duck. Frustrated, he began barking at the floating bird.

"Looks like he's standing on the end of a soft diving board," Dave snickered.

"I forgot," I explained. "He's never entered water from anything but solid ground or a boat blind. I knew there'd be some comedy in this program sooner or later."

As much as I encouraged Gunnar to go ahead, he wouldn't enter the water. He stayed put, oscillating on the fringe of leatherleaf, barking at the dead ringneck.

"Well, let's try this," Tom said, flipping a dead tree branch toward the duck.

Gunnar saw the splash. Now, wanting to go more than ever, he knelt down on his front elbows and, rear end in the air, slid into the lake like an otter. We all shouted encouragement as he resolutely swam across the water and retrieved...the stick.

"Good boy," I told him as he struggled back on the floating bog. "Now bring me the stick." Triumphantly, Gunnar brought me the branch. He sat at heel, and I took it from him, feeling—but not looking at—the two smirking faces behind me.

"Now," I told Gunnar, "if your uncle is through playing let's get to work." I gave him a line again and whispered "Back!"

This time he bolted for the water and only slowed down at the water's edge before tiptoeing into the drink. "Not much of an entry," I admitted to Tom and Dave, "but under the circumstances, I'll take it."

Gunnar returned with the first bird and then went after the second, bringing both to hand.

In the next couple of hours the three of us each burned a dozen shells, only managing to down four more birds before deciding to call it quits. "This is harder than shooting sporting clays," Dave commented. "At least Gunnar didn't miss any."

He was giving the Lab a left-handed compliment for the last four retrieves. The comical antics of Gunnar's first try had obviously been forgiven. His later retrieves weren't difficult ones, except for a diving cripple, but they were pretty to watch.

The following year, a hunting trip found Gunnar and me in South Dakota on the Hunter's Moon. When we arrived home, I thought it too late to find ringnecks on the bog lake, but we went anyway.

It was an unseasonably warm afternoon for late October. Still, I was surprised to see two dozen ringnecks loafing on the water when we slipped through the bog's cordon of spruce. The ducks took off when the dog and I emerged from the cover of the trees, but I didn't shoot as they flew overhead. No hurry, I mused, they'll be back.

I sat down and leaned against a lichen-covered tamarack. Gunnar posted himself in the leatherleaf and sat facing the sun, absorbing some of the last solar warmth that would grace this place for several months. It was solemnly quiet.

Bogs are archaic habitats, their plant assemblies as old as Cretaceous. And even though this bog couldn't be older than the glacier that retreated over this spot ten millennia ago, it had to be at least a thousand years old. It was a little spooky to think that in that time Gunnar and I, and Dave and Tom, may have been the only hunters to visit this wilderness lake.

A bog lake doesn't like change, at least in a time reference meaningful to humans. It remains essentially the same from one year to the next. In the few years I had been coming here, though, my life had changed. I'd started a new career. One of my daughters—it seemed they were still little girls only a couple of years ago—would be beginning college soon, the other leaving the country for a year as an exchange student. Friends, family had gotten older, moved away. Some had died, others had borne children—the cycle goes on; time and events continually change us.

Here at the bog, however, there is an aura of constancy. This is a place, a feeling, I need. It is a private place for Gunnar and me, a place where we can go and he'll always be a puppy, dangling over a blowdown, his little legs thrashing the sweetly redolent autumn air. He's a grown dog now, and we have hunting memories of other places and other times. Here at our ringneck lake, though, we share something special, not only with each other but with the ducks and the trees, and with the ancient mosses and frost-browned heather.

We sat for a long time without seeing any ducks. A bald eagle soared high over the bog twice, inspecting the water—searching, no doubt, for a fish near the surface. Ducks hate eagles, and I knew the big raptor would be seen by any ringneck heading back to the lake.

Finally, the eagle departed and ducks started to return. Gunnar saw them first. I noticed him gazing intently over the trees behind me.

A half dozen birds zoomed in over the trees off to my right. I grabbed the shotgun and eased into a kneeling position, waiting for them to complete a counterclockwise sweep of the lake.

They continued around the bog and circled toward us, heading, apparently, for the water directly in front of me for a landing. On they came, closer, never wavering, then feet down, wings cupped, braking the onrushing descent, sunlight reflecting off their bellies. I shot only once, killing the lead drake from the small flock. He tumbled dead on the water, raising a brilliant, sun-glittered explosion of water.

"Back, Gunnar!"

The dog, to my surprise, actually leaped off the edge of the bog and started swimming toward his prize. He surged across the dark surface, webbed feet and muscular legs stroking hurriedly. He'd grown stronger, had matured since our first visit here.

Gunnar brought me the dead ringneck. I held it awhile, admiring it. As I did, a small, tear-shaped drop of blood oozed from the tip of its bill.

Slowly, pensively, I gazed around the peaceful lake, then gently wiped the blood from the duck's mouth and slid it into my game pocket. Gunnar sat watching me, his bright yellow eyes following the bird as I tucked it into my coat, then staring up into mine.

"C'mon, pal," I murmured, "let's go home. Sometimes one duck a day is enough."

SONNY, GOOD NIGHT

by E. Donnall Thomas Jr.

B y virtue of an unwritten rule I've never understood, writers aren't supposed to discuss the deaths of the dogs that have served us. Retrospectives are permissible, as long as they read like biographies with little or no direct reference to the terminal event itself. There are justifications, of course; elegies are by nature sentimental, and the distinction between the sentimental and the maudlin represents a slippery slope indeed. But death awaits every hunter as surely as it awaits every quarry, whether the hunter walks on two legs or four. Thirty years of medical practice have left me painfully aware of the disservice we do ourselves and those we love by avoiding this obvious fact until it's too late to appreciate its implications. After thousands of pages of prose devoted to the easy subjects—shooting and retrieves, companionship and training, sunrises and wild places—I feel ready to test the limits of the envelope. I hope you do, too.

NINE

It never really occurred to me that I'd spent a dozen years writing the chronicle of my yellow Lab Sonny's life, but every time I sat down to record my thoughts about some recent episode in the field, he seemed to be there. When the subject was ducks or pheasants, the explanation proved obvious: he was there, virtually without fail, from the time he arrived in the household as a wriggling pup right through the bittersweet years of his dotage. But he also managed to worm his way into stories and essays that had little if anything to do with wingshooting.

Some attentive readers reported that they felt they knew Sonny better than they knew me, which may reflect my own instincts for privacy more than my ability to create the portrait of a Labrador retriever, even inadvertently. Fact is, Sonny was always a hard dog to escape, and I never felt like making the deliberate attempt necessary to edit him out of every corner of my life.

My photo file remains to prove the point. I'm still surprised to see that broad, blond muzzle peering back at me every time I put a page of slides on the light box, even when the ostensible subject of the photographs was fish or bows and arrows or the kids. He always seems to be laughing quietly at a joke that went right over everyone else's head. Now that he's gone, I wish I'd taken more time to learn what he was laughing at, but that's the kind of realization seldom achieved until too late.

In fact, his sense of humor may have been Sonny's most valuable asset. It certainly wasn't his marking or handling ability, as I was always the first to admit. In all our years together, I never really managed to get mad at him, despite occasional pretense on my part in the aftermath of some particularly aggravating transgression. I just couldn't do it, and neither could anyone else. Even the most rigid of my hunting companions (not that I have many of that kind) quickly learned to accept Sonny's shortcomings and enjoy the show. Of course, Sonny maintained an uncanny sense of timing that always resulted in a brilliant retrieve just as everyone was ready to write him off for good, but in retrospect I wonder if my friends were simply listening for the punch line of that obscure canine joke themselves.

ᘐ

One August day last year I came downstairs early in the morning and found that Sonny couldn't stand up. We'd been expecting something of this sort for some time, since the dog was fourteen years old and had shown signs of declining health for several years. Long retired from the field, he'd somehow lost part of his tail, depended on his nose rather than his eyes to recognize family, and negotiated stairs by way of a hopping, rocking-horse gait that seemed to require careful consideration of every step. My wife, Lori, and I had discussed putting him down on several occasions, but Sonny demonstrated no evidence of discomfort, wagged the remains of his tail furiously at any excuse, and continued to demonstrate obvious signs of pride in the completion of his daily routine, even though his job description had largely been reduced to slow, methodical tours of the house in search of the optimal place to take a nap. I even continued to throw a dummy on the lawn for him every night, although he usually forgot the point of the exercise soon after the command to fetch, leaving me to complete most of these retrieves myself.

But his condition that morning was qualitatively different. Instinctively, I reverted to clinical mode—I still practice medicine in my other life—and welcomed the brief moment of emotional detachment this change in perspective provided. Sonny lay with his head tilted unnaturally to the left, and when I wrapped my arms about him and raised him to his feet he consistently collapsed to the same side. In medical terms, he demonstrated focal neurological signs, and those aren't good. I didn't need an MRI scan to tell me he'd suffered a major stroke overnight.

By the time I'd carried Sonny out to the garage and placed him on his favorite sleeping pad, I wasn't feeling much like a doctor anymore. I brought him his water dish, but this gesture was more for my own benefit than his, and he was honest enough to decline the offer. "At least his tail still works," I pointed out to Lori, who stood red-eyed by the door. A nurse herself, she ordinarily would have been busy making professional efforts to fix things, but this time she recognized that whatever happened next was fundamentally between the dog and me.

I was supposed to head to work soon, but work, for once, could wait. Oblivious of the shed hair carpeting the pad, I lay down beside Sonny, closed my eyes, and let the steady rhythm of his tail wagging against the pad lull me into an unrestricted flood of memories that I made no attempt to direct. Sonny gave no indication of discomfort, anxiety, or regret, and I had to wonder if somewhere behind those clouded brown eyes he was reliving those same memories, too.

Despite his admitted technical flaws as a gun dog, he'd enjoyed a stellar career in the field, largely as a result of desire, determination, and opportunity rather than talent on his part or meticulous training on mine. Sonny loved the water and received his sternest tests there hunting mallards on local spring creeks during our late season, with subzero temperatures the rule. His sheer enthusiasm under such demanding conditions earned the respect of everyone who hunted with him and more than made up for his occasional handling lapses. And he could have written the book on one quirky element of duck hunting over moving water: keeping track of fallen birds in strong current. When I think about Sonny as a water dog, I'll always remember him best cutting across creek bends, calculating angles like a defensive back running down a receiver, and returning with a greenhead most dogs would have lost to the stream. Field-trial tests don't measure that ability and many superbly trained dogs never master it, but after a dozen seasons on the creeks Sonny could have given lessons to any of them.

Despite these abilities, it was upland game that really brought out Sonny's best as a gun dog, again as a result of heart and experience rather than talent or training. As the popularity of versatile retrievers has grown, a body of well-intended instructional literature has grown with it. But the fact remains that no advice can substitute for on-the-job training in the development of a flushing retriever. Living in the middle of pheasant country, we enjoyed abundant opportunities to hone our skills on wild roosters as a team, and Sonny easily translated the lessons he learned on pheasants to sharptails, Huns, sage grouse, and, at some point in his long career, just about every game bird in North America. If I could summarize his life afield in one snapshot, that image would show Sonny bulling his way out of a tangle of thorns with a live ringneck cradled in his mouth, glancing up as if to say, "Bet you never thought I'd run this one down!" In fact, I never doubted it for a moment.

ᜫ

But as I lay beside him in the garage—smelling the old dog smell from the scruff of his neck and listening to his tail slapping against the pad like a metronome—nonhunting moments began to dominate my emotional stew of final impressions: His endless patience with the kids, whom he helped raise from toddlers to hunters. The uncanny accuracy with which he greeted arrivals at our country home, barking protectively at strangers and burying his muzzle warmly into friends. The wake of chaos that followed his wagging tail through the house, as anything and everything stored at dog level crashed to the floor. His ability to distinguish shotgun from longbow as I prepared to leave the house in the dark (the first always led to an excited scrabble of claws on the hardwood floors, while the second earned looks of disappointment sufficient to break any heart). His one ill-advised attempt to prove Labs tougher than cougar hounds, a false impression that Drive, his longtime kennel mate, quickly corrected. His determined enthusiasm for mud, and the dingy canine paw prints that appeared in countless unlikely places after every rain. Never mind the ducks and pheasants, the flushes and retrieves. I was losing a best friend, not a hunting machine.

Finally, it became impossible to delay the inevitable any longer. As Lori retreated in private sorrow to the house, I carried Sonny to the wooden dog box in the back of the truck and tried to pretend we were going hunting. My usual vet was out of the office and I hadn't met his new young partner before. But he was an avid hunter and gun dog enthusiast, and knew of Sonny by reputation. We spoke longer than we had to about dogs and all they meant to us, and his empathy afforded me a badly needed measure of calm. Finally I carried Sonny into the clinic where the vet examined him briefly. "You're a doctor," he said. "I'm sure I don't have to explain what the head tilt and gait disturbance mean."

"I understand," I replied.

"And you're comfortable with the decision?"

"As comfortable as I can be."

He arranged syringes and needles and shaved the back of one of Sonny's forelegs. I'd thought like a physician once that morning and once was enough. I didn't even ask about the technicalities, the dosages, and the contents of the vials. I said good-bye, and it was over. Sonny's composure and the young vet's compassionate style lent an element of dignity to the act that I never would have imagined possible. As I carried the dog's lifeless body back to the truck, I wondered if my ability to help my own patients' families through the deaths of those they loved was equally effective.

Back at home, Lori and I stood in a long embrace without speaking, because there was nothing to say. I removed Sonny's collar and fastened it to the right main beam of a whitetail rack mounted in my office, where it remains as a reminder of what matters and what does not every time I sit down to type. Then I carried Sonny out into the yard and buried him.

Life does go on, although not nearly as easily as some would suggest. I remember sitting in a darkened movie theater back when I was a kid, palms sweating and stomach churning as *Old Yeller* built slowly to its grim climax. In typical Disney fashion, the moviemakers tried to soften the impact of that final rifle shot with images of a frolicking puppy and strains of upbeat music at the end, but I wasn't buying it. "That kid just had to shoot his dog!" I remember thinking. "This is bullshit!" I knew it, and every kid in the movie theater knew it too.

But there really is no cure for the loss of a beloved hunting dog like an attempt at replacement, a fact all who care about dogs and can't imagine life without them need to accept. Thanks to the peculiar rhythms of our biological clocks, we're going to outlive all our dogs but the last one. Sonny replaced Sky, just as Sky replaced Bogey—each marking a decade or so of my own life with his own unique style and character. In fact, "replace" isn't really the proper verb, for nothing can truly replace an individual. But each chapter in this gradual succession of Labrador retrievers did help fill the hole left behind by the end of the last, and introduced me and my family to a new set of talents and idiosyncrasies sufficient to form the substratum of yet another canine chronicle. Labs go on as surely as life itself, even when individuals have left us.

Rocky had just turned two when Sonny died, and it already seemed clear that he had the talent to exceed his predecessor's accomplishments in the field. And while he's integrated himself just as surely into the fabric of life around the house, it's fascinating to note the differences in the two dogs' personalities. There's a workmanlike quality to Rocky's loyalty. While Sonny remained an implacable extrovert, ready to jump into the arms of anyone willing to scratch his ears, Rocky prefers to follow me quietly everywhere I go like an eighty-pound yellow shadow. At the end of a retrieve, Sonny always made it clear that his job was done the moment he delivered the bird, but Rocky will ham endlessly for the camera, posing patiently like a professional model. In fact, to those in tune with the nuances of canine personalities, dogs are every bit as different as kids and just as challenging to decipher, hence the inaccuracy of describing any of them as replacements.

That's why there will only be one Sonny, and I'm not ashamed to admit how much I still miss him. That leather collar, comfortably worn down by years of cold water and warm sweat, still reminds me of all the unique attributes that made him a dog instead of a tool. And one day perhaps it will help me understand the private joke that informed his every action, and show me how to laugh at it, too.

TRUST IN BLACK

by Ted Nelson Lundrigan

Though he slay me, yet will I trust in him...
(Job 13:15)

"**D**oes this dog have a name?"
The middle-sized black Labrador retriever was snuffling its good morning into my hand. The dog had come up the wooden steps, in the dark, with its handler. Square headed, with a thick otter tail, he had stood for a moment, looked things over, and, seeing me dressed in plain green and standing alone, walked over to say hello. I was the doc, and he was the scout dog.

We were separated from the others, sitting together on the perforated steel planking of the helicopter pad—just he and I—leaning against my rucksack. About forty feet away in distance, but in a world apart of their own, clustered seven tiger-striped Army Rangers in the early light of another morning in South Vietnam. A machine gun, stacked against other packs, glinted against the flat seacoast sky. The bright end of a cigarette, glowing from the shadow of a face under a floppy hat, lit the ammo can as a belt of cartridges was drawn out in a picket fence clatter. The housekeeping chores of war.

"Yeah," the handler said. "He has a name. It's Oscar Peterson."

I hadn't laughed in a long, long time. It rolled out of me. In a morning where nothing was funny and things were bound to get worse, I threw my head back and, after a few suppressed clucks, gave up and hooted. A bright line of white teeth grinned back as a wet black nose knocked the glasses off my face. Labrador retrievers love a good joke.

"OK, OK," I said, as I wrapped my arm around his neck and pulled the dog against me. I had found a kindred soul in a strange land.

"I just call him O. P."

"Thanks, man," I said. "What do they call you?"

"Pete Hanson."

We shook hands.

Old soldiers don't like replacements, especially ones who come in alone. For five days I had been shuffled from airfield to combat base, starting with a jet airliner in the south, a cargo plane to the north, and then by truck even farther north to a man-made anthill outside a town called Quang Tri. Along the way I had been issued my basic bundle of helmet, cloth cover, belt, cartridge pouches, canteen, and rucksack, along with some bad meals, a bird's-eye view of a rolling countryside, and finally a bunk in a tent. When I woke up the morning before this one I had looked out on a parking lot with big green trucks and concertina wire, stacked up and stretched out, Slinky style, in front of watchtowers and bunkers. It had been Thanksgiving, but I missed my turkey dinner. The mess sergeant pushed me out of the chow line because I had no unit. He couldn't credit the meal and he wasn't "serving no G–damn orphans!"

I had walked back to my bunk in the replacement tent, thinking "can't get much worse than this," but it did. My midafternoon nap was interrupted by a grumpy clerk.

"Don't sleep with yer boots on!" I sat up and put my feet on the plank floor. "The captain wants to see you. You a medic, ain't cha?" Not waiting for an answer, he said "Follow me." And I did what I was told, being from the Midwest and all.

In that part of Vietnam, and in all the parts I was to be in, there were two constant elements: the "whupping" sound of helicopter blades and red dust. Old soldiers had a rusty patina. The weave of their clothes and the pores of their skin absorbed the fine, reddish air until it became a second color. Months later I would be standing in a busy terminal far south of here and, without my saying a word, a flight clerk would look me over and say, "The plane for the DMZ is over at Gate 5." I got to looking around as I walked to my door and, sure enough, every rusty-colored soldier was headed in my direction, thin red men in a sea of green returning to the border country between North and South Vietnam.

The officer seated in front of me could have been a barn. "Doc, you won't be here long, but I've got you now, and I need a medic for a patrol tomorrow. My usual guy rotated out yesterday. He'll be gone about three to five days. I'm putting you with some Rangers and a scout dog. Should be no trouble. Any questions?"

"Yessir. I don't have an aide bag."

The captain pointed to a box in the corner. "You can have my doc's."

"I don't have a weapon."

"Pick one out of the rack in that corner," he replied, gesturing to another part of the room. "Anything else?"

"No sir."

"Good. The corporal will show you where to go. Be on the pad at 0530."

I was going to salute, but the captain was looking down at his papers and waving good-bye.

"Here's the aide bag and a chit for your dinner and breakfast. Pick out a weapon, and follow me," said grumpy. And once again, I did what I was told, with one nonregulation difference. I spotted a Model 12 Winchester riot gun in the rack wrapped in a bandolier of green high-brass shot shells. This was something I could understand and take comfort in.

I had seen other dogs in Vietnam: The usual native ones with the mandatory curled tail, quarreling around the food dumps; some fortunate ones of the same ilk serving as soldiers' pets; and the massive, 100-pound-plus German shepherd sentry dogs that patrolled the perimeter of the airfields. The Labrador was a complete surprise. O. P. was the same happy, tail-swinging, clownish duck boat passenger that I had spent my last leave with. Except for the fact that he and I, and his handler, were about to fly off this steel-planked pad in a helicopter, we could be going on a bird hunt. I even had a shotgun. On the other hand, the shells may have been green Remington plastic high-base, but they contained small steel arrows in a black granular matrix. "Fléchette rounds" the clerk had called them.

O. P.'s owner was dressed in olive green, like me, and had a cloth-covered steel helmet and a M-16 carbine. He had added words as decoration to the camouflage pattern. The letters on the elastic band around his cloth cover read: "Freedom's just another word for nothing left to lose." Our other hunting partners weren't dressed in duck hunting camouflage. They wore black-and-green tiger stripe to blend into a country that had no golden swamp grass.

A lanky figure separated from the Rangers and walked over to us. He knelt down on the decking and spread a map out flat, then turned on his flashlight.

"OK guys, here's the deal. Doc, you stay with me and the RTO [Radio Operator] at all times. Hanson, you and your dog will take point. We are going to scout Route 9 from the old firebase called Vandegrift, where we will land, up the Quang Tri River valley, to the Khe Sanh plateau. We'll bend left, go around the old airfield, and finish up at Lang Vei under the shadow of the old Special Forces camp. We're looking for mines, booby traps, bunkers, and anything else that has shown up since last time. We'll mark them and blow them. Mostly, we stay on Route 9, the old highway, unless something comes up. Any questions? Load up. The choppers are on the way."

Route 9 was made famous in the 1968 seige of Khe Sanh. That fight had ended in April that year. It was now November 1970, and the Marines had left the base to the jungle. Route 9 technically connected the coastal plain of South Vietnam by passing through the forested hills and mountain meadows of the Quang Tri River valley until it climbed the steep east side of the Khe Sanh plateau. There it split into a Y, with one branch going north along the river valley until it narrowed into a tumble of rock and trees, and the other continuing west past Lang Vei and on to Tchepone in Laos. The coastal segment of the road was currently used for the supply of Camp J. J. Carroll, an Army mountain stronghold, and for access by armored units in their occasional raids to shoot artillery from Vandegrift and the Rockpile, both former

Marine bases, now abandoned. Beyond Vandegrift, the once busy highway had returned to the jungle, far different than the highway it had been in French Colonial days.

Hindsight being 20/20, I can tell this history to you now. But at the time I had never been to any foreign country other than Canada. For me, in that place at that time, the whole world consisted of the two Huey "slicks" descending on us. Mrs. Lundrigan's well-behaved, clean-cut, bird-hunting boy was about to go to war.

Pete and O. P. climbed into the first Huey, and I climbed into the second chopper and pressed against the back wall of the cargo bay. On one side of me the radio operator stared ahead, and on the other the patrol leader was giving full attention to his map. One more Ranger sat in each doorway, with feet dangling out above the countryside of Vietnam. The ocean was on the right, with a new day's sun showing the water's straight line. The mountains were on the left, and below us we saw a narrow ribbon of highway. We were headed north, and from Quang Tri there is not a lot of the South half of Vietnam left.

It was all forms of movement: engine noise; thwacking, vibrating blades; wind pouring through the open doors; and the ground, zipping by at first, then seeming to stop altogether as our two helicopters reached cruising altitude. Sometimes we would rise up on an air bubble, drawing alongside the other chopper. I could look into the doorway.

There, silhouetted against the bright new day, were O. P.'s head and shoulders. For a while I could imagine that I was still on the little river that flows into Egg Lake, with my duck boat behind the other, and the two of us pushing our gear and dogs through the channel. It was a good thought. I ran my hands up and down the contours of the Model 12 between my knees, as I had done then, and remembered…it had been only three weeks ago.

၃၅

It may seem improbable, but I slept. I was awakened when the chopper went into a steep bank, and I lifted up off the floor while my stomach went the opposite direction.

"Lock and load! Remember, stay low and move front and away!" I pushed six green shells into the magazine.

The deck raised up and—with a thump and a bump—the skids hit ground. I followed the radioman and, in a gust of wind and dust, we were on the red grassy remains of Camp Vandegrift. Just like that, both birds were gone. In their place I could hear some insect noise, a metallic voice on the radio, and my companion's response.

The hills rise up around Vandegrift. If we were the cavalry in an old western movie the Indians would be making smoke signals from one peak to the other. My little patrol was smack-dab in the bottom of a rock and grass roaster pan.

But nothing came of it. The bugs chirped, the radio squawked on and off, and the grass swished as I walked through it, shifting the rucksack to the middle of my back and the aide bag to my left side, and tightening the bandolier of shotgun shells around my waist. In addition to three more canteens of water and three days' rations, I had a green towel around my neck, a poncho, a poncho liner, and a folding shovel. Within three yards I had sweated through my fatigues, which did not dry up until the day I left that place. We pressed on to the roadbed of Route 9, where I paused, removed my helmet, and tied a rolled-up kerchief around my head. Up ahead I could just make out the round top of Pete's helmet and sometimes, the happily swinging tail of O. P., a Labrador retriever at war. German shepherds look like war, and Doberman pinschers look like death itself, but a Labrador retriever, in any place, is still the happy kid thinking a rock fight is a ball game.

The army selected Labradors because they had better noses than German shepherds or other breeds. The Labrador scout dog was a trouble detector, not a fighter. Whether it was metallic wire, metal buried under the ground, plastic in the trees, or the body scent of an ambush, the Lab could find it. The army got all that with the Lab and more, at no extra cost...to them. A Lab never quit. His batteries never ran low. His sensors never clogged or failed. The only job I had was to keep moving. O. P. had to move

147

and search, watch out for Pete, listen to him, and listen to everything around him. It wasn't until the first break that I remembered to jack a shell into the riot gun. O. P. didn't make mistakes. On the other hand he did eat my C ration pound cake and peaches.

"C'mon, Doc. You've got to save that for yourself," said Pete, who had finished his C rations and was tearing up the box to bury it. "O. P. don't care if it's hot chocolate or lima beans and ham." O. P. stretched out between us, panting into the ground, his tongue lolling out on the red dirt. As I scratched his ear I looked around.

We had crossed over the Quang Tri River at the point where the old French Bridge had been. Its steel girders still showed a graceful curve crossing the air above the water to tie back unto the other side of the valley. It had been blown up years ago. We rested in the shade of the big rocks. Three of the Rangers talked quietly, three stood watch, and the patrol leader talked into the radio.

"How is it going for O. P.?" I asked Hanson.

"Fine," Pete answered. "Nothing so far. We found some boot tracks, a dud RPG rocket, and a 60mm mortar round. That's about it"

I reached out and stroked O. P.'s side. "He's a good one," I said "Seems strange to see a black Lab in this place."

"He's better than those other army dogs," said Pete. "So far he's saved my life twice. Once, he stopped me before I walked into a booby trap string. There was a grenade in a tin can on either end. One time, after that, he sniffed up three Bouncing Betty mines and a buried, and fused, artillery shell in this same road." Pete gestured toward the elephant grass meadow across the river. "Little sumbitches are probably watching us right now. They know about O. P., and he knows about them."

"Where you from Pete?"

"Arkansas," he answered.

"Did you train O. P.?"

"Nope. Army trained him. I'm his second guy. When I leave he'll get another one like me. He'll be here for keeps. No going home for O. P." Pete's voice cracked a little.

"Why not?" I asked. "You'd think the Army would have some sort of retirement. You know, find him a good home or something."

"Nope, O. P. is dead. Yankee dogs get some sort of disease over here and they all gonna die. No going home for O. P." A black nose pushed under Pete's arm and two merry brown eyes followed. "Don't mean a thing." Pete was in pain, and O. P. had to look out for him.

The patrol slowed down, for this side of the valley was new territory. In some places the tree limbs were bent over the broken paving rocks and tied to bushes on the other side. There were side tunnels, too. The patrol leader pointed to an opening in the elephant grass along one side. The grass had been tied at the top to form a roof for a narrow trail. We waited. In a minute or two, the rustling of the stems could be heard moving our way. I half raised my shotgun, but it was only O. P. returning from a cast down the grassy tunnel. Pete's small frame followed, with his helmet slung on his belt, and the M-16 carbine slung across his chest.

Pete hooked O. P. up to his lead. "They been here," he said. "Not today, but in the last couple of days. Three sets of tracks. One leading, two carrying something heavy. They come this way, to the road."

Smack, smack, smack. The slapping of O. P.'s tail against my leg bought him the head scratching he wanted. But for the serious side of this, I thought, we could be Boy Scouts on a hike. Bait a cane pole, catch a fish, and make us a camp. Yee haa.

Pete and O. P. moved back up to the front, their feet raising little puffs of red dust that lingered in sunlit patches, but drifted back to the ground in the shade. The pair of them eased around the corner of the old route where it bent out of the hillside. The colonial road builders had cut into the face of a down-sloping ridge to make a sharp left-hand turn open to the river below yet straight sided to the earth above. A bad spot. The part around the switchback corner was out of sight. Ahead, the road clung to the hillside as a dark, interrupted line against an alpine meadow of waving elephant grass.

The Ranger point man, second in line to O. P., eased down to one knee. He stared ahead for a moment, then shifted his

M-79 grenade launcher to his right hand. Every one stopped. The fingers on his left hand said, "Wait....one...minute."

The hand said Pete and O. P. had found some game.

So I waited. At first I stared forward, then down. Drops of sweat flickered for a moment in the air between my nose and the ground. Then they would hit the dust, puffing like water on a hot stove. Little explosions.

I felt it before I heard it—something like what happened when I was washing my hands in a bus station rest room. I had been a little uneasy about the neighborhood, it being a big-city place to my small-town life. I had turned quickly to get a paper towel, and wham! I was seeing stars and my glasses were spinning into the sink. I was stunned and instantly furious. I jumped back to swing at my attacker, and saw that I had walked into the towel machine.

It was like that. One instant kneeling, the next slapped in the face and chest. Then I heard it. It was not a Hollywood-movie-John-Wayne-deep-two-tone boom. It was a flat crack of lightning with no resounding thunder, just a drifting cloud of gray smoke and red dust. When you are lying on the ground, tight to it, the little rocks are uncommonly big. Several were still rolling between the point man and me. So was Pete's helmet—round and round it spun, on its top, nothing left to lose.

The squad leader ran forward with the radio telephone in his hand and the RTO went with him, pulled along by its cord and with his antenna waving in the red air. I followed the two of them, past where the point man had been and around the corner—out of my old life and into my next one.

Friends, I'll tell it to you now, and it's a true thing: The eyes can see, the limbs can move, but the mind will not allow the soul to comprehend what it sees. If this were not so, then a rational man would seize his ears in both hands, draw up into a fetal position, abandon hope, and scream in horror.

My new and only friend, Pete, had been laid open like a slaughterhouse pig.

Where the road joined the earth bank, in front of him and to one side, a smoking hole was all that remained of a buried mine. Up ahead, laid out like roadkill, was O. P.

"C'mon, Doc! C'mon, we gotta go!" The point man held up a string of electrical wire. "Command detonated mine! Somebody's watching us!"

"Go?" I hollered. "He's still alive! If we move him he'll split in half!"

I pushed the coils of Pete's guts inside the biggest field dressing I had. Then I tied a second dressing around his back. His pack was gone, his carbine was gone, and so was most of what holds a human together. I wrapped him around the middle with an elastic bandage.

"Doc, we've got to move. This is too open. I'll get your poncho out. We'll dump him in it and go." Spoken quietly right into my ear, the point man's words provided an island of calm in chaos. As quickly as I had finished, the Rangers had Pete in the middle of my poncho, one of them on each corner, and were hustling their load back around the corner.

Rolling up my aide kit, I reached for my shotgun. I wanted one last look at O. P. He was moving his head! Then he raised it and looked directly at me.

I called to him, slapping my leg. "C'mon, O. P.! C'mere! Let's go!" He didn't move.

I looked back at the corner, where the two Rangers were waving to me. I knew they wanted me to get back, but I looked at O. P. a second time and, impulsively, ran to grab him.

"Doc! Stay away!" they yelled. "He's telling you there's another mine!"

Too late. O. P. looked up as I slung the shotgun around my neck, grabbed him by the scruff of his neck and the loose skin of his haunches, turned about, and carried him around the corner where they had pulled Pete into the shade. The Rangers formed a perimeter around us.

The radio was cracking with the patrol leader asking for a med evac and waiting for news. Pete was awake and screaming with the pain. Before we left I had stopped by the 18th Surgical Hospital for some advice and a bottle of plasma, which I had taped on the strap of my aide bag along with a tube and needle. The remedy was as old as war, but was something of a trade-off. Pete needed lots of fluids to ward off shock, and saltwater Ringer's Solution would have been better. I went with plasma because the bottle was lighter and smaller to carry, and was supposed to make up in content what it lacked in quantity.

I got him hooked up on the first try.

One of the Rangers held Pete's head. "Can you give him some morphine?" he asked.

"Nope, no morphine for gut wounds." I turned to the RTO, asking "Can we get a dust-off in here?"

"Not here, Doc. The CO says it's too steep. We've got to find a flat spot near the top."

"That won't work. He's awake now, and every bump will be agony."

A cascade of red dirt balls and rocks tumbled down next to us followed by the patrol leader. "We've got to take him up hill, Doc. The dust-off can't fit on this hillside."

"If we move him, he'll either go into shock from the pain and die, or start bleeding inside and die."

"Doc, listen to me," the leader grabbed my shoulder and pointed uphill. "There's a little flat spot up there. It's not far. We've got good cover. And one other thing, the bad guys are on the road behind us."

Another Ranger joined in: "There it is, bud. We're going up."

"Fine, I'll put him to sleep. Let the hospital docs sort it out." I inserted the needle sticking out of the end of a small gray tube of morphine into the plasma line and squeezed it. Then, I took the red grease pencil out of the aide kit and marked Pete's forehead with an M.

"Pete," I spoke loudly. "Pete!" He opened his eyes and looked into mine. I'm gonna put you to sleep. We got to move you."

Pete gestured for me to bend down. I took off my helmet and put my face next to his. O. P. was all he said.

"He's right here beside you," I answered, and put his hand on the dog's neck. O. P. raised his head and laid it on Pete's chest.

Pete pointed at me. "O. P.," he said. "Take care of him, Doc. Wasn't his fault...dummy mine in front...drew me and him in."

"Yeah, man. I'll get him, now good night." I inserted and squeezed a second tube into the plasma line and Pete closed his eyes.

The same four Rangers picked up their bundle and started to climb.

I grabbed the leader's arm. "What about the dog?"

"What about him?" he answered.

"We can't leave him!" I said.

"Doc, I'm not risking the lives of my squad for a damn dog!"

"I'll take him!" I pleaded.

"Fine, but you better keep up, you understand?"

"Yeah, I understand."

I threw my rucksack and its rations down into the river gorge. Then I lay down on my back with my neck against O. P.'s belly and the back of my head behind his ribs. I draped the shotgun sling around my neck—over one shoulder and under my right arm—so that the gun would hang in front of me. O. P.'s front legs were in one hand and his back legs in the other.

"OK, boy. Let's hope for the best." I rolled over on my belly and raised up at the same time. O. P. didn't even grunt. He was draped around my neck like a sack of grain. I started to climb, letting go of the dog's hind legs from time to time to grab a sapling and pull us up. We ran out of trees, but not out of hill. My legs were burning and shaking, I wasn't going to make it.

"That didn't last long," I thought. Suddenly, my feet were light and I was lifted across the ground by strong hands holding on to my web belt. The last two Rangers covering our climb had added my weight to their climb. The tall grass separated, and O. P. and I were dropped onto a pebble-covered outcropping. Pete lay on the poncho, pale but breathing. O. P. lay still also, looking up into my face.

"Dog," I said. "You gotta move or one of us isn't walking out of here. C'mon, O. P. Stand up!" I pulled him to his feet, but his hind quarters just fell over, followed by his front legs.

"What's the matter with him?" asked the RTO.

"I don't know. He has no holes in him. Maybe the concussion stunned him or broke his back." I moved my hands over his body, feeling for something out of order. Everything was there, but nothing worked. He just lay with his mouth open, panting.

"Dust-off is on the way, Doc." That brought me back to the real reason I was with this bunch. I checked Pete's pulse: it was weak, and his skin was gray and clammy.

"Stay with me, Pete! It's all gravy after this!" Months later a wounded soldier would turn to me and say. "Doc, if I'm gonna die, I don't want to until this med evac gets here, 'cause he's so slow I'll live forever." But he wasn't dying and he knew it. He had been hit in the left cheek of his butt and, while it was a hard place to tie a bandage, it wasn't a fatal wound. Unless the bird got to Pete within the next five minutes he would be gone.

I have never understood war movies. Hollywood heroes sneak across the sky in UH1 Huey helicopters. In truth they are as noisy as a kid running along a picket fence with a stick. But nothing ever sounded so good. We could see him and talk to him on the radio. He was coming in.

The bad guys could see him too. Sir Charles was no idiot. The med evac choppers were piloted by the best officers in the corps. That is probably all that saved him. He came in hot and low, never made a pass, just bored right in. The Rangers scooped up Pete, I grabbed the plasma bottle, and (I'm sorry, Pete) we threw him into the open door. The chopper medic caught the IV bottle in midair and they were gone.

The air crackled around us, but the North Vietnamese Army was downhill, and it's hard to bring the bullets to bear shooting uphill. It was time to duck and run.

I still had the problem of what to do with O. P.

I wanted to think about it some more, so I figured there wasn't a lot of damage I could do to him greater than what had already been done. This time I just grabbed him on the run and slung him over my shoulder. Adrenaline is a gift. I didn't lead the pack off that hill, but I can tell you more of them were behind me than in front.

Pete had been hit in the late afternoon. We had almost gained the lip of the Khe Sanh plateau, and by climbing straight up we were now on flat ground. The far side of the plateau is bordered by a ridge—an ancient, flat-topped butte. The map, now spread out in front of all of us, showed that between where we were and that ridge was an old rubber plantation.

"We can make this old plantation house by dark," the leader said, tapping the map with his finger. "I've been there before, the fire bases have it zeroed in if we need help. Doc, what are you gonna do with that dog?"

"Carry him, if I have to," I said. "Why can't we call in a chopper and fly the hell out of here?"

"Dust-off pilot said they are socked in with rain and fog at Quang Tri," he answered. "No ordinary chopper will be coming up that valley—maybe not for a couple days."

"It's ten clicks [kilometers], Doc. We aren't stopping till we get there, and you can bet the little people are not far behind us." No one said another word. It wasn't an embarrassed silence, just a long pause.

O. P. wasn't looking at us. He just lay on his side, quietly, staring at a grown-up row of rubber trees.

"Oh, man," I thought. "O. P., somewhere in a better world your blood cousins are swimming for ducks, lying in front of a fire, eating well, and sleeping late. There's mallards in the flooded oaks, pheasants in the corn, and grouse in the aspen. Here you lie in a rotted-down jungle of rubber trees, busted up and hurt, trusting in me to do the right thing, and ready to call it the right thing no matter what I decide."

"Can't shoot him, Doc," said a quiet voice. "The noise will bring them down on us." They were all shadows again. The same as this morning, but now they were friendly shadows.

"I saw some phenobarbital in this bag," I said. "He'll just go to sleep."

They stood up, all at once, and each walked out from me, like the spokes of a wheel. Then they sat down, each with his back to me, weapons aimed out.

I unbuckled the aide bag. The two small parts unfolded. I unzipped the big compartment and, by touch, found the hypodermic cylinder, slender and long. It dropped neatly into a metal holder with a ring-topped plunger. I set the bag aside, laid the shotgun on top of it, took O. P.'s hind leg in my hand, and uncovered the needle. The big artery was easy to find, and he didn't even feel the sting. I drew back on the plunger slightly, got blood, and slowly closed my thumb and two fingers. Right at the end—like a lot of brave dogs, and like all of my Labrador retrievers after him—he rose up slightly, then gave it up.

I held him for a while—maybe a minute, maybe longer. I felt a hand on my shoulder and a quiet voice in my ear said, "Let's go. There's no moon tonight and we've got ground to cover."

"We can't just…leave him like a carcass," I protested. "Not a dog like this. He saved our lives."

"We're not gonna just leave him, Doc. He won't be wasted."

I didn't understand, but before I could ask the question the leader said, "Cully, fix it up."

A short, squat figure came out of the gloom, digging into his rucksack as he walked up. "Just move along, Doc. When I'm done setting these charges under O. P. those little bastards will have cold cuts with their rice." He kept humming and chuckling as he set the trap. I followed the others, single file, walking between the RTO and the leader, like a good little army dog.

About ten minutes later there was a vicious crack-flash. I didn't look back, but I had a thought: "If I ever get out of the pesthole alive, I'm going to treat every black Lab like a gift from God."

The rain and fog came in after midnight and lasted until just before dawn. I was huddled in a borrowed poncho under the shelter of a spiral stone staircase. It was about all that was left of a French rubber plantation house. Its graceful curves would have made a complete turn within three floors, if the floors had been there. The others had let me sleep until the last radio watch. I sat and stared at the black dials and white numbers, one little red light telling me that some part of the world was listening back. Under the spire of a chimney, across the rubble-strewn floor, was the front of the grand fireplace. It gets cold up here in the mountains, I thought. A fire would have been good.

"Take a break, Doc." A dirt-smeared hand pushed a ration can of cold spaghetti and meatballs into my shoulder. I nodded and walked over to look at the stone mantel above the mouth of the fireplace. There were figures cut into the face of it. Hunters shooting ducks and dogs bounding to retrieve them. Labrador retrievers. Dogs chasing stags. I wonder where they went when all this happened?

"Doc?"

"What?"

"Want some Tabasco sauce?"

It was Cully. He put a small red bottle of the foot soldier's friend into my hand.

"Doc, don't worry about what happened. It don't mean nothin'."

The Vietnam grunt's anthem. And after a while, it didn't. They flew us out of there. In two days I had orders for my next stop. I was to be one of six medics for a self-propelled artillery battalion...right on the DMZ. The good news was that there would be no more patrols, no more black Labrador scout dogs. No more running through the jungle.

The bad news was that in February 1971 my whole battery moved up Route 9, across the Quang Tri River and up onto the Khe Sanh plateau. I rode a tank right past where Pete and O. P. were blasted into doll rags. It was just a muddy depression on the roadside. Four weeks later I would ride a helicopter back over the plateau and down the river valley. Looking out the door, I saw the orderly rows of rubber trees and then the curled spiral of the stone staircase. I remembered Black Labrador Scout Dog Oscar Peterson (O. P.), and it meant something.

It's been more than thirty years since I clung to the red earth of the DMZ and the soft black fur of a brave army dog. I have raised, hunted, and trained two black Labradors, one after the other, each into old age. I tried, in every way I could think of, to keep my word to Dixie and Jet, and they, in turn, filled twenty-five of those thirty-something years with accomplishments that could be recited here, though not without bias, because I'm hardly an impartial witness.

I haven't gotten into another black-haired trust for the past five years. I just can't stand it anymore. To be there when their clocks run out is too hard. So I hunt ducks with my German shorthair. He's not great, but he's fond of me. He wades thoughtfully into the potholes, avoids snags, swims fairly well, and finds his way back. We get by and, more important, he's a pointing dog. He occasionally doubts that I know what I am doing, and I return the favor. After all those years of being right, all the time, a little less trust is probably better for both of us.

ALL GHOSTS AREN'T WHITE

by Mel Ellis

B ig water with its weird white fronts of fog does things to men's minds, and forgotten tales sometimes take on substance away out where the gulls fly patrol. Perhaps that is why men on the oreboats that ply the Great Lakes docked with stories of a big black Labrador, with a duck between its jaws, swimming through the mists many miles from any shore.

Sober men might have wondered what sort of rations the oreboat men were being served if it had not been that others also claimed to have seen the dog. Duck hunters fought snow storms back to shore to tell of a huge black dog, its muzzle white with frost. Commercial fisherman untangling nets said they'd seen the Labrador swimming through heavy seas, and they all claimed the dog had a duck between its jaws.

It was eight years since the first fisherman docked at Wisconsin's Fish Creek Harbor in Green Bay to ask if anyone had lost a Labrador as "big as a Shetland pony and black as midnight." I was stowing gear aboard a big boat for an island hunt and walked over in the twilight to listen.

"He stood on the point of Treasure Island and he had a duck in his mouth," the fisherman said. "We whistled but he couldn't hear me on account of the roaring surf. Then we edged in as close to shore as we dared without going aground, but he ducked into the brush. And yet there were no duck hunters out there today."

The next morning I combed Treasure Island with a friend whose name must even remain a secret; we'll call him Jerry. Treasure is the largest of the Strawberry group. We found huge imprints in the sand where a dog had run the night before. Thinking that maybe the animal had crossed to another island, we spent most of the afternoon searching three rocky outcroppings nearby. We killed a limit of gold-eneyes while doing so, but found no further trace of the dog.

In Milwaukee that night, I looked in the classified advertisements—and there was an ad promising a reward for the return of a black Labrador "lost on the Strawberry Islands."

Next morning I phoned the man who had advertised and told him what I knew. For obvious reasons, I'm not going to reveal his name, but will identify him only as R. J. H.

"That's Jeff, all right," he declared. "I wouldn't give a penny reward for him if I didn't know a guy who'll buy him as soon as I can get a rope around his neck."

As I hung up the receiver, I hoped R. J. H. wouldn't get his dog back. I didn't know exactly why I felt that way, but somehow he chilled me.

Next day I called Jerry. I started off by telling him about this R. J. H. who had lost his dog. "You haven't seen that Labrador, have you?"

"What did you say the man's name was?" Jerry asked.

I repeated the name. "Know him?"

There was a long silence. Finally Jerry said that he did, that he had guided for the man once, but that he'd never let him set foot on one of his boats again. I wanted to go into it further, but long-distance telephone calls cost money, so I figured to take it up with Jerry the next time I saw him. After I'd hung up, I remembered that Jerry had forgotten to say whether or not he'd seen the dog.

On a hunch, I phoned the editor of a field-trial publication. He knew the man and told me about him. Said that while judging a field trial he had disqualified the fellow for abusing his entry.

That afternoon I shot some pigeons for a retriever trainer named Chuck, who lived north of Milwaukee. He knew the man, too—had trained the dog for him. "And what a dog!" he said. "One of the most promising youngsters I've ever seen."

"What about the man?"

Chuck frowned and talked reluctantly. But between his story and the editor's I could piece the picture together.

Evidently, here was a dog completely loyal to a man, who gave him nothing but abuse.

Chuck told me he'd asked the man to leave his place after he'd kicked the dog for failure to remain steady on the line. "But the dog stuck to him," Chuck said. "I've seldom seen retrievers take that sort of treatment and keep coming back for more. But that was the kind of dog Jeff was. Once he set out to do a thing, he stuck to it until it was done—whether it was making a retrieve, whipping another dog, or licking this guy's boots. You figure it."

I couldn't, so I forgot about it until about a week later, when the man who had lost the Lab called again. He wanted to know if I'd heard anything further. I told him I hadn't and—intrigued by now—asked him how he'd lost the dog.

"The fool went out after a goldeneye and just didn't come back," he said.

"Just didn't come back?" I repeated incredulously.

"That's what I said," R. J. H. replied. "The duck was a cripple and he followed it. I whistled, but he kept going."

"But," I said, "you went after him in a boat, didn't you?"

"Not on your life I didn't. It was blowing. I wasn't going to get wet. Water was coming over the gunwales and it was freezing."

"Oh," I said, and hung up.

I had the picture now, and it wasn't a pretty one. The man had been hunting a small island north of Treasure Island.

The dog had never heard the whistle above the pounding surf. Intent on completing the retrieve, Jeff had become lost out among the big waves and eventually wound up on the wrong island.

I felt sure someone would pick up the dog, but three weeks later, it was apparent that no one had, because the man called me again. "I think somebody is keeping my dog," he said.

"Maybe you're right," I agreed. "But how are you going to prove it?"

"Oh, I can prove it if I can locate my dog. I've got my initials R. J. H. tattooed in his left ear."

Winter came in quick that year. I didn't hear from R. J. H. again, but the following spring and summer I heard rumors of a big black Labrador being sighted in the vicinity of the Strawberry Islands. It wasn't until fall, however, that an Associated Press story came across my desk quoting a commercial fisherman as saying he'd seen a Labrador as huge as a small horse on the shores of Treasure Island—a dog carrying a duck.

It was a good story as such stories go, but I threw it in the wastebasket. For one thing, I didn't want R. J. H. to read it. Not that I believed the fisherman, but some people might. And a good newspaper doesn't encourage the circulation of stories having no basis in fact.

Less than a week later one of our correspondents sent in another story telling how three duck hunters had seen the big black dog silhouetted against an early-morning moon on the rocky point of the island, staring out toward the open water. He was still carrying the duck.

This time I couldn't ignore the story. State papers were picking it up. Nobody believed it, but to them the apparition was symbolic of the perfect retriever roaming endlessly through a world of water and sky with no thought but to complete his retrieve.

That winter R. J. H. kicked one dog too many and was brought to the court for cruelty to animals. This was the first time I'd got a look at him, and I didn't like what I saw. That made it still more difficult to understand how a dog could give so much love and loyalty to a man who deserved it so little.

I finally filed big Jeff's love for R. J. H. in the same pigeon-hole in which would be filed the love story of a woman who follows a no-good husband straight through hell to be by his side. It was one of those things you don't figure out—just accept.

I wrote and told Jerry what had happened to R. J. H. A night or so later he phoned me and spent nearly ten dollars in toll charges telling me how he figured R. J. H. had got just what he deserved. That wasn't like Jerry, so I wondered after he'd hung up why he was so concerned over the fate of a man he guided but once.

For six years, then, the stories kept coming in. Sometimes bass fishermen would see the dog on a summer evening as they fished the reefs that ring the islands. The year the lake trout started to make a comeback, anglers bobbing through the ice told of a black dog trotting across the frozen horizon, carrying a duck in its mouth.

It made intriguing copy unless you knew about R. J. H. and then it was kind of sickening. A score of times I was tempted to write the true story of how he'd deserted the dog. I figured the animal had starved the first winter; no dog could survive on those bleak islands. But when you're a newspaperman, you never forget the law of libel, so how could I write about a scoundrel who'd abandon his dog to the elements? How could I write about a dog that had given his heart to a man who didn't deserve it?

I even searched for the animal's bones one spring while up bass fishing. But the islands have many bones of gulls and of crippled ducks that crawled ashore to die, of animals washed ashore, and even of Indians. I found no clue.

Several times, I dropped off to see Jerry, but he was always out fishing. Then one fall there were no more stories about black ghost dogs, so I checked with the Associated Press and they put a query on the wires. I called our correspondent on the lakefront, and he talked with a score of duck hunters and commercial fishermen. But no one had seen the dog for nearly six months.

I supposed the story had just sort of worn itself out, that men had wearied of hearing it and that those who visited the Strawberries didn't see the dog now because their imagination had no news-story stimulation. In a way, I was happy about it. It was one story I was content to let remain half written. I hadn't seen R. J. H. in years, and that was all right too.

I hadn't seen my friend Jerry either, and I was happy to get his call to come up to the islands for a hunt. "The goldeneyes are down this year, like they've never come through before," he said.

He knew that would get me. Shooting goldeneyes when they come whistling down from the Arctic with icicles goosing them all the way is a sport comparable to none. You hunt the big water and you fight ice on the decks, and waves coming over the gunwales, and snow in your eyes.

Jerry's dogs greeted me. There must have been six or eight in the kennel in back of the house, and they roared a welcome when I drove in. It was good seeing Jerry again after all those years.

After dinner, we sat in the living room, and it was then that I noticed the big Labrador on the rug beside the chair.

"Going in for house dogs?" I asked.

Jerry laughed self-consciously. His wife had never let him bring a dog into the house. "This one is retired. I retired him about six months ago."

Six months ago? I couldn't help remembering that it was just about six months ago that the last of the "Black Ghost" stories had come across my desk. I wondered. Jerry had retired lots of dogs in his time, but that hadn't meant they could come into the house to wait their lives out. I knew there was more.

"Good dog?" I asked.

"The best," Jerry said.

"Had him long?"

"Quite a while."

"Buy him from someone around here?"

Jerry nodded. "In a way you might say I did. Bought him, that is."

I leaned over then and flipped the Lab's left ear so that the initials R. J. H. were visible.

Jerry shifted uneasily in his chair. "To be honest with you," he began.

"You don't have to be honest with me," I interrupted. "Just tell me, when did you find him and did he still have the duck?"

Jerry walked over, knelt, and took the dog's graying muzzle between his hands. "I had him the very first night you called. I was about to tell you—I intended to tell you—but then you mentioned the name of the guy who'd lost him. I knew then I'd never tell anyone."

The Lab's tail beat a soft sound against the rug.

"Did he have the duck?" I asked.

"He had a duck. I don't know if it was the one he was chasing the day he got lost, or a cripple he'd picked up. You know how hard it is to kill goldeneyes. You know how the crips are always coming ashore in a blow. It might have been a crip."

"But." Questions crowded my mind. "How about the villagers, the hunters, the fishermen?"

Jerry scratched the dog's muzzle gently. "I knew they'd be looking for him. But I'd see Jeff dead before I'd let that louse get him back. So I locked him in my island-fishing shack. He broke out a couple of times. Some of the oreboat deckhands and hunters must have seen him. Maybe he was even picking up cripples. I suppose that's how the stories got started. Then, just before the big freeze, I brought him home."

The big dog sighed. I sighed too, and as a man turns the final page of a long, long book, I turned the big Lab's ear down to hide forever the initials R. J. H.

IN LOVE OF THE WEE FECCHEN DOGS

by Michael McIntosh

s I am the twig my father bent, I have always been an upland hunter. Had his passion been for ducks rather than bobwhites, mine probably would be, too. As it is, occasional forays for wildfowl shine like crystals in the matrix of memory, but my heart belongs to the uplands.

I learned to hunt over Dad's last pointer, a lovable, hard-driving old girl named Cookie. Among other things, she taught me the ineffable thrill of seeing a dog on a solid point—and then, to complete the circle, fetching back whatever fell to the gun.

"Fetch." Interesting word, derived to our idiom from the Middle English verb *fecchen,* which in its turn evolved from the Anglo-Saxon *feccan,* or in earlier form, *fetian.* In any guise, it means "to go after and bring back." But *fetch* also has an adjective form that is the equivalent of *charm.*

To be fetching is to be charming. To be charming is fetching. To be a retrieving dog is to be a charming fetcher, or a fetching charmer. Or whatever. Either way, it feels good to a hunter's heart.

When the time came for a gun dog of my own, a pointing breed was a foregone conclusion. Much as I love watching English pointers work, I had a rare moment of good sense and decided that I couldn't do justice to the task of trying to train a really high-powered dog amid the demands of graduate school and starting a teaching career. So I opted for a Brittany, a breed that struck me as rather more laid-back.

Some are, some aren't, as I found early on. All Brittanys seem to have the sweet nature endemic to the breed, but after struggling with a couple of wild hares, I decided to do some research in preparation for the next one instead of just snagging a good-looking pup out of a litter.

I still get angry when I think about what I discovered— namely that certain bloodlines have been developed specifically so Brittanys can compete in field trials alongside pointers and hard-going setters. Which to my mind is precisely the opposite of what a Brittany was meant to be—gutsy, of course, but more genteel in the way the dog works. Covering three counties in half an hour is not the Brittany way, or shouldn't be. It's like stuffing an ounce and a half of shot into a 20-gauge shell and thinking you've somehow improved its performance. If you want to shoot a 12-gauge load, shoot it in a 12-bore gun. And if you want a dog that performs like a pointer, get a pointer.

So I searched around and finally found a litter descended directly from the oldest Brittany blood in North America, with nary a trace of the hotshot genes that have done more, in my opinion, to degenerate the breed than improve it. She came from Minnesota, and we weren't even halfway back home to Missouri, with wee October First sleeping all curled up in my wife's lap, when I got the feeling that I had something special.

Indeed, I did. She grew through her puppyhood all too soon. Then she changed from being a leggy, gangling teenager into a classically beautiful specimen of the breed.

I knew she could point—first captive quail in my pasture and then wild birds—but what I didn't know until she was about two was that I didn't really have a pointing dog. I had a retriever.

I've always been of a mind with my father, who insisted that all of his dogs retrieve. It's become a quaintly old-fashioned idea now, but in Dad's day, and in the formative years of my life as a hunter, a pointing dog that didn't retrieve was only half a dog. So Tober and I played endless games of fetch, both indoors and out, graduating finally to my hiding something somewhere in the house and then telling her to go look for it and bring it to me. She loved it.

So far as I can tell, Brittanys are natural retrievers, especially those of older bloodlines. Tobe became living proof. She had a reasonably good nose, though by no means the

TWELVE

best I've ever seen, and she had the Brittany tendency to want to get nose to nose with the birds. That was OK for quail and woodcock and pheasants in thick cover, but she never quite mastered ruffed grouse. Chukars—birds that seem to have no instinct to hide—drove her bats. If she held a point on three chukars in her whole life, I've forgotten about two of them.

But what she lacked as a pointer, she more than made up as a retriever. I have hunted over every standard sort of retrieving dog plus a few oddball breeds, and good as some of them were, there wasn't a single one, of any breed, against whom I would have hesitated to back Tobe for any amount in a contest of find and fetch.

Here's how good she was: We hunted for twelve seasons and hunted hard, for both I and my knees were younger then. In those twelve years, we lost exactly one bird, and that one was my fault, not hers. I wing-tipped a grouse in Minnesota, thought I knew right where it was, and kept calling Tobe back in whenever she started to cast more widely. If I'd had my wits about me, I'd have realized the bird was running and the dog was following foot scent. That one got away. But nothing else ever did—dead, wounded, in timber, brush, grass, you name it and she had it sooner or later. It took a while sometimes. I once sat on a log in Minnesota, puffing my pipe for fully ten minutes while she unraveled the trail of a winged and moving grouse, caught it, and brought it to me. Another time, I dropped a quail dead in the middle of a huge brush pile. Tobe rooted around for a few minutes and came up empty. We passed the same spot about half an hour later, and with no prompting from me she dived in again, rummaged around, and finally came out with the bird.

You can't teach that sort of thing. You can only admire it.

As I understand it, Brittanys are not supposed to be water dogs. Tober apparently forgot to read that chapter in the book of *How Things Is Spoze to Be Done.* (I sometimes suspected she skipped the chapter on pointing, too, but that's another story.)

She loved water and would literally break thin ice to get into it. I'm sure the affinity was natural, but I'm also certain that I helped develop it by exercising her in my neighbor's pond every day during the hot, muggy Missouri summers. She'd go paddle around on her own just for the hell of it, but if I tossed her little canvas dummy out to the center, she'd make a beeline for it as fast as she could swim, grab it, and bring it back. Eight or ten such trips every evening kept her muscles in good trim, while she stayed cool besides.

She didn't have the coat to withstand cold water and chilling wind, but I took her duck hunting a few times during our September teal season. She never did grow fond of sitting still in a blind, so I had to keep her tethered, but she'd go after a duck on the water like gangbusters. She fetched a few quail out of farm ponds and lots of grouse and woodcock out of swamps—and to all appearances, loved every minute of it.

TWELVE

∽

Lots of Tobe's retrieves come to mind, some stand out. It was late on a gloomy, mizzling, Minnesota afternoon. We were by ourselves that day and wound it up with a turn through a lovely piece of cover separated from the road by a hay field. We moved a couple of birds, and I shot one of them. In the end we trudged up the hay field edge toward the car, both of us pretty soggy and Tobe more or less at heel. The last hundred or so yards was along a year-old clear-cut, the popple sprouts nearly as high as my head and thick as cat hair. Tobe suddenly trotted ahead and spun into a solid point. I walked up to her, and a grouse flushed from about fifty feet inside the regrowth. I shot it, it went down, and Tobe bored in. It occurred to me that from her perspective she couldn't possibly have seen the bird either flush or fall. I was just lining up my mark, preparing to wade in and help, when she came out, soaking wet, carrying a dead bird in her mouth.

I assume the bird had been puttering around right at the edge of the popple and had scuttled deeper in when it saw or heard us coming—leaving enough fresh scent in the damp air to catch Tobe's attention. Through the entire sequence I did not speak a word. Her confidence in my shooting, learned from the dozens of release-box quail I had shot for her, was as touching as some of her retrieves were astonishing.

∾

Quite a few of my hunting partners had Labs, who inspired my tremendous admiration for their versatility, keen intelligence, fearlessness, and occasional buffoonery. My good friend Ted Lundrigan's retriever Dixie probably found, flushed, and fetched more ruffed grouse than any Lab in dogdom. I hunted with her the last few years of her life and could tell you stories to take your breath away—but those are Ted's stories to tell. Suffice it for me to say that I've never met a sweeter, more willing old girl.

Burly, on the other hand, is one I can tell some stories about. He belonged to another of my pals. He fit his name perfectly—a big lad of about eighty-five pounds, strong as an ox, and sometimes just as stubborn. Burl would hunt anything. Ducks, geese, quail, pheasants, doves—it was all the same to him.

He also would eat anything that didn't eat him first. He was especially fond of roadkill of any variety, dead fish, and other such disgusting things he might find. I once saw him swallow a dead squirrel—and I mean swallow it whole, tail and all. He was amazing. Trouble was, his digestive system wasn't quite up to his appetite, and no hunt was complete until Burly had barfed up about ten pounds of some god-awful stinking mess in the back of Jim's station wagon.

Burly was a teddy bear with people and a gunslinger with other male dogs. Some of his battles were epic—like the time at a service station on the Pennsylvania Turnpike when he climbed into a car filled with people and one German shepherd, and proceeded to whale the crap out the shepherd while people fled from every door like rats from a burning corncrib.

Nor did he tolerate any disrespect from game birds. Jim and I were hunting pheasants in western Iowa one time, working along opposite sides of a little creek bottom. A rooster came barreling out on my side, I made a sloppy shot, and the bird scuttled, broken winged, into about a quarter-acre patch of tall grass. Burly and I had been together enough that he'd readily hunt for me, so I asked Jim to send him over and directed him into the grass.

I could follow Burly's progress by watching the grass, and presently a great commotion broke forth, followed by an outraged yelp, followed by silence. In another minute or so, Burly emerged with the bird and trotted up to hand it over. He had a bright trickle of blood on his muzzle and, I swear, a grin on his face. The pheasant probably didn't have one intact bone left in its body; it was like hefting a feathered sack, limp in every direction. Pick a fight with Burl, and you'd better be armed with more than a set of spurs.

Another time, also hunting pheasants in Iowa, Burly ran into a string of barbwire hidden in the grass of a fencerow, and laid open a flap of chest hide half the size of my hand. That was beyond field first aid, so we went back to the car and found the local vet.

The examining room was about the size of a closet, and it was a bit crowded with four hunters, the vet, and his assistant, to say nothing of Burly. But a moment after the vet started trimming the edges of the skin flap with scissors, everyone—assistant included—suddenly disappeared. I'm not put off by that sort of thing, and in fact insist on being present when any of my dogs undergo a surgical procedure. So I held Burly to keep him flat on his back while the vet trimmed and stitched. Burly neither flinched nor even twitched through the whole thing. That was the day I became convinced that Labradors are born without nerve endings.

I have plenty of evidence, however, that they are born with an inordinate quantity of gray matter. For several years I was chief gun for the Missouri Valley Retriever Association. Let me tell you, it's tough duty to stand there all day and shoot pigeons or flighted ducks, but it has its rewards—mainly in the opportunity to watch a lot of retrievers work. I saw a few whose performance was virtually heart-stopping; a lot who turned in a workmanlike job; and some who, by virtue of inadequate training or insufficient genes, shouldn't have been there at all.

I thoroughly enjoyed the experience and would do it again in a heartbeat, but it also taught me that a trial dog and a gun dog are not necessarily the same animal. The successful trial dog will, of course, follow a straight line, regardless of what's in the way. A successful gun dog will—or should, in my opinion—use its head and follow a line that conserves its own energy. The result is the same, a bird in the hand, but wear and tear on the dog will nearly always be less.

I know several guys who have bought retriever-trial washouts and got splendid gun dogs. As best I can tell, a washout is a dog that's too independent-minded to become an automaton, or one who can't hack the stress of a training regimen measured largely in amperes. And don't sneer at the so-called soft dog. How many of us have difficulty coping with stress? Call that a rhetorical question, but ask yourself honestly why a dog should be any different.

Now, it may sound as if I have a woody for trial-dog trainers. On the contrary, I admire them. They work their butts off without getting much in return. They do it because they love working with dogs. My beef is with those who design the trials, who keep moving ever and ever farther from the real world of a hunting retriever. I don't expect to be invited to judge a trial—and if I were, I know damn well I'd never be invited a second time. The gulf between trial dog and working gun dog grows wider every year, and to be candid I think that's a disservice to the animals.

If you want to meet a dog that will never come within sight of a trial, stop by my house sometime and meet Goldrush Kate. I'm not even sure she'll get within shouting distance of being a good gun dog. As I write this, she's about to enter the "terrible twos," as puppyish now as she was a year ago. Some of the best field-bred golden retriever blood ever developed courses through her veins, and she is unutterably beautiful and endlessly affectionate. Katie is also extremely bright and for the most part biddable—but she just hasn't decided that it's time to grow up. On the other hand, neither have I, so I'm not inclined to be too pushy.

Why a golden after thirty-odd years of Brittanys? Several reasons. Old Tober died in September 1998 at better than fifteen years old, and the loss just burned me down. Twelve hunting seasons and three years of retirement forge some bonds between a man and a dog that cannot be broken overnight, if ever. I'll never reveal what I said to her in the last hours of her life. But I held her in my arms, the old girl too weak to even raise her head, while Dr. Larry Stoddard found the vein. As the light went out of those lovely, expressive amber eyes, her message to me was not an invitation but a promise. She is waiting for me in some distant place. It's my job to find her.

Two years, the psychologists say, is the typical time frame for the grieving process, and it was two years before I could even think about having another dog. I no longer live in Missouri. Here in the mountains of South Dakota I have neither a good place to train a pointing dog nor access to the captive birds I'd need. Besides, both knees and one hip are showing signs of heading south, and I'm not sure I could keep up with a pointer of any breed. I've always liked the golden's personality. They seem to take to the life of a house-dog a bit more readily than Labs, and they don't have the Lab's naturally oily coat. I'm one of those who believes that over-frequent bathing is hard on a dog's skin.

Having a retriever has been a revelation. Pointing dogs are on a continuous quest, just as they were bred to be. In this terrain, getting lost could take about thirty seconds. Now that Katie's reached something like adult age, she's not quite the stick-at-home she was as a puppy, but she'd still rather be close to me. It's a rare thing if she gets a hundred yards from me on our daily rambles in the higher country. Fifty is more like it, and when she reaches that she either sits down to wait for me or comes bounding back as if to wonder why ol' dad isn't keeping up. Try to explain knees and hips to a two-year-old dog. Easier to try explaining base-ball to Martians.

I frankly don't know when she'll develop the mental discipline for training more serious than the play-fetching we've done since she was forty-nine days old. Actually, I don't know that she ever will, although I assume so. There's something in those deep, gentle brown eyes that promises as much for the future as Tobe's gaze was grateful for a long, long past.

Either way, though, it doesn't really matter. Regardless of what happens, I'll have an utterly sweet companion, and I've reached an age when that's more important than just about anything else. I doubt she'll ever be called upon to fetch any-thing in the face of ice floes, turbulent rivers...lions, tigers, or bears. She has the heart for hunting under those conditions, but I don't. More likely, she'll learn to scoop pheasants and sharptails out of stubble or short grass. At those times, I reckon we'll feel pretty good about ourselves and each other. Heroics are for the very young, those whose task is to dis-cover the value of one-sided conversation as the car rolls through gathering dusk—conversation that turns on the memory of having done our respective jobs, however sim-ple, neatly and well. What we say is for neither broadcast nor publication. It is as privileged as what passes between a man and his wife, for it's all spoken in the language of the heart.

WHY OTHER PEOPLE
PICK OUR PUPS

by John Barsness

M ost hunters are deeply influenced by their hunting mentors. Mine were both "edible generalists," hunting every kind of game that tasted good. They were not strict meat hunters, for both gloried in the ways of nature, but they were practical men who used what worked. Both favored Labrador retrievers, the dog that hunts anything.

I watched the Labrador evolution with one of the men. After high school Norman Strung moved to Montana from New York City and became friends with my father, one of his university professors. At first Norm had pointing dogs, but he eventually found they weren't exactly right for some Montana hunting. At one point he used a pair of Brittany spaniels to point upland birds, keeping a Lab at heel for the tough retrieves. He eventually noticed that his Lab often slipped away and flushed pheasants behind the Brittanys. Since Norm also loved waterfowling, the choice became easy.

My other mentor was an old Dakota Indian named Ben Burshia, born in 1898. Apparently he also went through a succession of hunting dogs, though by in the 1970s, when I met him, he'd settled on Lab crosses. I knew two of these, one female and one male. Apart from Lab they apparently had coyote and rodeo bull DNA in their genes, though apparently this beat the hell out of some dogs Ben had owned. He was particularly down on Chesapeakes, as he had once had a huge male so stubborn that Ben once used his cattle-roping skills to drag the dog out of the pickup.

During this period I was wed to Ben's oldest grand-daughter. We didn't have much money, but I whined out loud about eventually someday owning a Labrador retriever. One day we drove to my mother-in-law's house and there, on the living room floor, were a pair of black Lab puppies. She told me to pick one. The smaller one seemed more lively, so I grabbed him. This is as close as I've come to personally picking the right pup in the three decades since.

For several complicated reasons we named him Gillis, and Norm gave me a copy of Richard Wolters' book *Gun Dog*. Gillis was six months old when bird season opened in September. By that time he knew most obedience commands and some basic retrieving skills. We'd also recently visited a house whose owner kept a parakeet. Gillis spent the entire time sitting under the cage, tongue out and tail wagging. As the decades have passed I've grown convinced this had more influence than my half-baked training.

On opening day we hunted a wheat farm where both sharp-tailed grouse and Hungarian partridge could be found around the stubble fields. Even at twenty I had observed that it was easier to hunt both birds a couple of hours into the day, rather than at the crack of dawn. At dawn they would be out in the fields and would often flush wild, but after the sun rose they would mosey into the crested wheat grass and wild roses around the fields, and hold better. Gillis and I hiked the edge of one field, and pretty soon his ears went up. I looked where he was looking and saw some sharptail heads in the wheat grass. Gillis ran toward them and the birds flushed, and I shot one with my grandfather's old Stevens 12-gauge side-by-side. Gillis ran over, grabbed the grouse, and brought it back. Holy smokes!

It went like that for the next thirteen years. Gillis grew into a seventy-pounder who could run all day. He once disappeared when going after a wounded pheasant and didn't return for over half an hour, the lively bird in his mouth. He also learned to dive for ducks. Once Norm and I hunted a local reservoir on a blue-sky morning. One drake mallard finally came by the decoys at long range, and I hit it too far back. The duck set its wings and sailed behind an island three hundred yards away. I got in the johnboat and rowed over with Gillis. We spotted the duck together, and it dove. Gillis jumped overboard, and for the next few minutes I got to watch a dog-duck dance underwater—resembling a slow-motion ballet except when both rose to breathe. Eventually I heaved Gillis and the mallard back in the boat, and we rowed back to the blind. Gillis lay on the bottom of the boat, ribs heaving as he caught his breath. As we rowed nearer, Norm asked if we got the bird. I started to answer, but Gillis beat me to it. He grabbed the duck and stood in the bow, showing off to Norm's younger dog.

I wasn't a very good dog trainer, but Gillis was a very good dog. He forgot some of the formal retrieving stuff, but learned to hunt anyway. When going after upland game he trotted along twenty-five yards in front of me, often looking back to see where I was headed. If I turned, he ran over and started hunting in front of me again. We didn't have to use whistles or collars because he understood that we were hunting together better than any dog since. He may have retrieved 1,000 birds in his life, of every legal variety in Montana.

In his last season Gillis was almost fourteen, as deaf and blind as a mineshaft, but he could walk level places and still smell some. When I took him out on opening day he found a covey of Huns alongside an irrigation ditch and I managed to hit one. It fell right in front of him and he happily slow-trotted over and picked up the dead bird—then kept walking. I ran up and grabbed his tail. He turned around and looked at me, puzzled, before a lightbulb obviously clicked on: "Oh, yeah! Now I put the bird in your hand." He caught a few other birds before the season ended in December, and died in January.

I had gotten remarried by then. Eileen had only known Gillis in his blue-fart dotage, but even to her the house seemed very empty. By spring we were making noises about another dog, perhaps a chocolate Lab because they showed up better in the photos we took for various sporting magazines. (Instead of looking like a dog-shaped lump of coal, brown Labs photograph more like a dog-shaped lump of, um...oh, forget it.) Norm Strung had purchased a chocolate through a friend, Tom Young, who had a good line on Labs, so we arranged to have him find us one, too.

We named this dog Keith, after the old Idaho hunting writer Elmer Keith. We had wanted another medium-sized Lab. Keith's parents weighed seventy and seventy-five pounds, but by the time he was four months old it was obvious that hybrid vigor had been involved. When hunting season rolled around he weighed eighty pounds, and he eventually topped out at nearly one hundred, none of it fat.

Where Gillis had been methodical, Keith was impetuous. Over the summer we taught him trout-stream manners. Gillis used to sit at the tail of a pool and try to catch water-skippers while we fished, almost reluctantly leaving when we moved to the next pool. Keith would sit quivering on the bank until he got the signal we were finished, then perform an enormous belly flop into the rainbow water.

THIRTEEN

Keith's early hunting style involved running until his head whacked a tree. He'd stop and shake his head, then stare at the tree as if memorizing exactly how big an object had to be before it could to stop him. Then Keith would take one step sideways and bull forward again. Something similar was the only way to really gain his attention. I'd whack him between the ears with the soft side of my fist, and he'd pick up his head and grin as if saying, "Gee, yeah, OK!"

He was an even better retriever than Gillis, and took hand signals extremely well—partly because I'd become a better trainer, but mostly because Keith was a natural. By his second season the three of us had perfected a method of pheasant-hunting the same trout stream. Eileen and I would walk each side, and Keith would bulldoze the heavy cover on the bends, crossing the river whenever necessary. He was a great goose dog, once running down a Canada another hunter had wounded an hour earlier. Keith found the goose half a mile away in a little pond, flushed it from under a cut bank, and grabbed it midpond. The first time we ever hunted from a waterfowl blind, he wormed his nose through the reeds and stared at the decoys, sitting absolutely still as a flock of one hundred Canada geese came in. He then made a double retrieve, the second from three hundred yards.

But when upland hunting, he was never as attentive to us as Gillis had been, though until the end of his life he loved to plow through thick cover (avoiding trees over 2.5 inches in diameter), which generally slowed him down enough for us to keep up. He was so big we couldn't hunt him except near water until late October, and he truly came to life only after the snow fell.

Keith started slowing down in his tenth year. We could remember how empty the house felt after Gillis left, and decided to go ahead and purchase a younger dog. Our taxidermists, a husband-and-wife team, had been breeding their fine female Labs for years. They were particularly careful about also finding hunting dogs as sires, so we arranged to get a pup from the next litter. This would probably be a yellow, and we decided on a female, as Eileen had had enough of life with a big, hard-headed male dog.

Over the years we'd read all about picking a puppy, and so we watched the litter closely. We finally picked a reddish-yellow girl that seemed lively and named her Druzilla, after Elmer Keith's daughter. She grew into a beautiful strawberry-blond dog.

I don't know what happened to Dru genetically, though we did eventually remember that one of Cinderella's evil stepsisters was also named Druzilla. Our Dru came from super hunting dogs on both sides, but acted like no other Lab I've ever met or heard of. She hated kids, and even if an adult human squatted to try to pet her, she acted like a Doberman after a burglar. If I changed hats she acted the same way.

But she was a retrieving fool. While training her we often went down to the Missouri River and tossed dummies into the faster currents. She never gave up, swimming almost as hard as Keith had in his youth. She loved blind retrieves and loved to play Frisbee.

She would retrieve anything except a dead bird.

We had started Dru, like Gillis and Keith, with pigeon wings on fly rods, then moved on to retrieving dummies wrapped in duck and pheasant feathers. She would snappily retrieve these on land or in water. But when the first planted chukar fell to Eileen's 20-gauge, Dru ran up and sniffed it carefully, then stood there looking at us proudly. We thought having Keith show her how would stimulate the connection. He did teach her to kill a wounded bird, but then she'd drop the bird and stand there, and quite proudly, too.

We consulted various trainers. This took a while, because all of them suggested the same techniques we had tried, especially gradually adding feathers and bird blood to the dummy. After we had thoroughly explained the situation, all of the trainers claimed they had never heard of such a thing, and some actively avoided us.

During this period Dru acquired another nonhunting habit that, depending on your perspective, might be worse than barking at her master every time he changed hats. In the mornings after both dogs had eaten, she'd follow Keith around until yesterday's meal had left his body. She would be waiting under his tail for a fresh, hot dessert. We tried all known methods here, too, with equally dismal results.

Near the end of her second hunting season, Dru had retrieved exactly seven birds. One was a leghorn chicken belonging to the taxidermists we had bought her from. We stopped one day to pick up a deer head, and Dru picked up the chicken, first chasing it into the chicken house. The egg crop was a little thin for a while.

She had also retrieved six pen-raised quail we had bought at the suggestion of yet another trainer. Eileen would take a bird from the cage, then loft it into flight while I shot. Dru retrieved every one, bringing them nicely to hand. Soon she understood the connection between cage and birds. After completing the last retrieve, she'd walk over to the cage and place a front paw on it, looking at us eagerly. All right!

Next we took her pheasant hunting on a friend's farm. The first rooster rose over the small river that divides the property. I dropped it cleanly, and it splashed into the drink and started downstream.

Lo and behold, Dru made a running leap into the water and started after the bird, putting up a wake like a small whale. Both dead rooster and orange Lab headed downstream rapidly, but Dru caught up just above the really fast water. She eagerly circled the bird, sniffing it thoroughly, then headed back to me. Once on the bank she grinned up at me, as if saying, "Yup, it's dead." (Luckily one of our friends was able to snag the bird as it drifted by a cut bank. She put the bird's neck in her mouth and waved. I offered her a job.)

We'd been putting so much effort into the retrieval deal I hadn't really noticed that Dru didn't much like to hunt, either. After the pheasant incident I suddenly realized that her "hunting" routine was to walk along a few feet ahead of me for 15 minutes, then plod behind, occasionally catching my heels with her front paws.

We put an ad in the local paper: "To give away, purebred yellow Labrador that will retrieve anything except a dead bird." The phone rang off the hook. We gave her to the first caller, a high school coach who'd always wanted Old Yeller. He and his wife had had an old beagle that had died and they wanted another house dog. They called a week later, totally happy. It turned out that the beagle had never been house-trained and they were astonished at Dru's good manners. They also had a hottub where Dru liked to swim. We figured Dru had been a Labrador-American Princess who'd always hoped for finer things than all that yucky bird stuff.

A month later we drove down to Arizona to hunt desert quail with our friend Web Parton, a bird-hunting guide, dog breeder, and dog trainer based in Oracle. He generally has about a dozen English setters on hand, along with a Lab or two for waterfowling. We told him our story about Dru and he kept shaking his head. He also fell in love with Keith, who had ridden along with us but was now too old to hunt seriously anymore.

We decided not to start another pup that year. Dru had been too much of a drain, so we would do a little easy hunting with Keith, but mostly concentrate on big game. Then in July Web called. It turned out there had been a party in the dog kennels one night, and his male Lab had impregnated one of his female setters. In fact, she had been pregnant when we had hunted over her in Arizona.

Of course she had eleven pups. Web had already given away nine, but he'd kept two, a female that looked almost like a pure setter and a male that resembled a yellow Lab. Web had intended to keep the male only until the two pups were six months old, as buddies for each other in the dog yard. He said, "You folks need this dog. He's a good boy."

Web is the gentlest dog trainer I've ever known, and thanks to Dru I've known a bunch. He hardly ever raised his voice above a whisper, and contrary to the common wisdom of giving dogs short, hard names like Mike and Kate that can be hollered loudly, he names them things like Alice or Lisette. Web has some of the finest dogs I've ever hunted over, so when he half-whispered that this dog was a good boy, we listened.

The good boy only cost us plane freight from Tucson to Bozeman. On the first of August, Byrd showed up after twelve hours in a dog crate, smelling awful and looking pitiful. We took him to the Gallatin River for a quick bath, and he lay at Eileen's feet on the pickup floor all the way home. It turned out that he didn't know anything except "no," not even his name or how to go up and down stairs. We didn't think Byrd was a particularly good name for a bird dog anyway, so renamed him Gideon, after an outstanding hunting guide we'd known in Africa.

In the first week we taught him his new name along with the come, sit, and stay commands, and Keith accepted him into the pack. Over the next three weeks we introduced Gideon to retrieving, water, and bird parts. He particularly liked chasing gulls and sticks at the local lake. He never caught the gulls, but became pretty good at fetching sticks, dummies, and dummies covered with bird feathers. He didn't look quite as Labbish as Web had implied, with a semifeathery tail that curled setter-fashion, four white feet, and white patches on his chest, nose, and tail tip. This was OK, because we'd learned the hard way that pretty is as pretty does.

The season started in September. I had an elk hunt planned in New Mexico, but before leaving we bought Gideon a few pen-raised chukars. He caught on quickly and retrieved four. While I was in New Mexico, Eileen took him hunting with some women friends and he caught his first wild bird, a sage grouse. His retrieves were tentative, but his lifetime bag of dead birds already exceeded Dru's.

After I returned elkless from New Mexico, we hunted Gideon on all sorts of upland birds, opening pheasant season on a wheat farm in eastern Montana. The first morning, we hunted the high grass between a wheat field and the Missouri River. Gideon sniffed along in front of me and then suddenly pounced. A rooster went up and started across the Missouri. "Well," I thought, while raising my old Fox, "here's where we find out if all that water work paid off."

It was an easy straightaway and I killed the bird dead in the air. By the time it splashed into the Missouri our new bird-mutt had flown off the bank from five feet above the water. He landed well out in the current and swam hard downstream after the rooster, clamping it instantly between his jaws. "Bring it here!" I shouted needlessly. He swam directly back and ran straight up an even higher bank where I knelt to greet him. He literally went flying over me, dropping the soggy pheasant at my feet and a gallon of river on my head, then he zipped into the tall grass behind me.

By the time I had climbed the bank with the soggy pheasant, Gideon was already two hundred yards out. Pheasants sprayed from the grass like grasshoppers from a July wheat field. By the time I had caught him a quarter mile later he was walleyed with ecstasy and I was laughing. By the end of the season the fever was under some control, and he was swimming half-frozen spring creeks to bring back mallards and teal.

THIRTEEN

In the four years since, Gideon has caught just about every legal bird in Montana, along with woodcock in Michigan, chukars in Idaho, quail in Oregon, prairie chickens in Nebraska, and geese in Alberta. He doesn't seem to have many pointing genes, but that's OK. I hunt all sorts of birds and mostly want a meat dog, as my mentors did. His personality is less hard-headed Lab and more sweetness and light, like his setter mother. One of our hunting friends first saw him in our car in the grocery store parking lot one day, and asked, "What kind of bird dog is that?"

The one thing we're certain of is that we're never, ever going to try to pick our own pup again. As with all of the good retrievers in our lives, we will wait for Fate and someone else to pick one for us. I don't even care if there's coyote or rodeo bull spliced into its DNA, as long as the dang dog hunts.

14

SOMETHING OUT OF NOTHING

by E. Donnall Thomas Jr.

Warm Indian summer air covered the marsh like a buffalo robe as the sun eased toward the western horizon. Insects buzzed lazily around the blind while the decoys rested quietly upon the polished surface of the pond. Somewhere in the distance a lone redwing called and its rich churr seemed to carry forever through the stillness of the evening. Waterfowlers accustomed to stinging winds and wave-tossed decoy spreads might be forgiven for feeling out of place, but it was October in Montana, duck season was in progress, and I couldn't imagine a place I'd rather be.

The delicious tranquility the marsh offered felt even more inviting than the remote promise of birds in the air. Bathed in warm golden light, the prairie rolled up and away from the cattails in welcome layers of emptiness as far as the eye could see. Except for a dissolving contrail way off to the south and a few rectangles of wheat stubble etched against the horizon, the landscape looked much as it must have looked to Lewis and Clark nearly two centuries earlier. After a long day of people and problems, I needed the respite the blind provided, every bit as much as I needed the ducks that might or might not arrive after all.

The absence of one's fellow man may equate with solitude, but it does not necessarily mean being alone. As I relaxed and settled into the process of scanning the sky, the rich aroma of wet dog filled my nostrils, gradually replacing the marsh's fertile stink. Standing at the threshold of his first full season, Skykomish Sunka Zee wriggled eagerly beside me on the blind's rickety wooden seat, a helpless victim of the universal adolescent longing for action now as opposed to later. As soon as I clucked at him he settled down, subsiding into a warm, wet presence against my shoulder. The remarkable thing, I remember thinking at the time, was how little space a damp ninety-pound Lab really occupies, even one whose manners have yet to be tempered by experience.

I've endured my share of evenings fretting over the absence of ducks, but this wasn't one of them. I'd spent a typical day at the hospital, delivering unwelcome news to people who deserved better and trying to derive some redemption from small triumphs apparent to no one other than myself and a handful of friends. I really didn't need to shoot any birds that night. What I needed was silence and the freedom it implied. But the instant I saw the teal skimming in low across the cattails I knew that we had them and I went into predator mode despite my contemplative mood.

Blue-wings can embarrass experienced shooters even under the best of circumstances. As soon as I rose from the bench the mud underfoot locked itself around my boots and gripped them like cement, which is my explanation for failing to convert the relatively easy double. By the time I dropped the first bird in the middle of the decoys, the flock had veered overhead, and when I tried to catch up with the second barrel I just couldn't twist around far enough to get the job done. As wingshooting excuses go, this one may not win any Pulitzer prizes, but that's my story and I'm sticking to it.

Despite all the long hours of training we had shared over the summer, I fully expected Sky to break at the sound of the first shot, but he surprised me. After offering a few choice expletives in the direction of the teal I'd missed and breaking the gun, I found the dog still sitting on the bench behind me. But as soon as I whispered fetch, he launched over the top of the blind and churned his way out to the fallen teal, which he scooped up like an infielder snagging a ground ball. Breathing heavily in response to a sense of urgency apparent to no one but himself, he ducked under the wire front of the blind and delivered the bird to my hand without ruffling a feather.

Technically, of course, there was nothing to the retrieve. A kid could have done it, and in fact a kid just had. And if I had been hunting without a dog, I still would have claimed that first bird, at no greater cost than a few minutes of effort and the possibility of wet waders on a warm night when damp feet hardly mattered. But as I helped Sky clamor back up onto the bench and watched him settle into position my intuition told me I had just witnessed a seminal event and that my life would never quite be the same again.

My intuition proved correct.

Let the truth be told: Under most circumstances, I wouldn't walk across the yard to shoot a duck unless I had a dog to retrieve it. Exceptions arise, of course, but they almost always involve the strong desire for a duck dinner in situations that preclude the presence of a dog. That's not waterfowling; it's shopping for food. There is a difference.

The retrieving breeds—especially Labs and Chessies—form such an integral part of the American waterfowling tradition that it's hard to imagine duck hunting's essential pageantry without them. There are practical considerations of course; no responsible hunter feels comfortable killing game that cannot be recovered, and dropping ducks in icy water without the services of a capable retriever often amounts to little more than feeding the local scavengers. All involved parties deserve better, especially the ducks.

But a good dog's company means far more than increased efficiency as a hunter-gatherer. For most novice hunters, the excitement of the hunt derives primarily from the shooting. But as the technical aspects of knocking birds out of the sky become more routine, the inquisitive mind naturally seeks other sources of fascination. There comes a time when an eager Lab's heart-stopping water entry or the tenacity of an experienced Chessie pursuing a diver with a broken wing serves not as a footnote to the hunt, but as the text itself. Despite our best efforts as trainers, dog work never becomes entirely predictable, and dogs always seem to find new ways to amaze and inspire us with their performance. The challenge of wingshooting may get new hunters into the duck blind in the first place, but it's the dogs that keep the fanatics coming back.

And they don't necessarily have to be dogs of championship quality. While I'm not involved personally with the field-trial circuit, I respect retriever trials for the standards they establish and the contributions those standards provide to the ongoing vigor of the retrieving breeds. Nonetheless, over the years some of the most memorable moments I've enjoyed in the duck blind have come courtesy of relatively unpolished retrievers that somehow found new ways to rise to the occasion. Tolerant attitudes like mine should not be construed as an excuse for intolerable behavior. No one enjoys hunting with an incorrigible hard-mouther or a dog that cannot sit still when required. The point is simply that wonderful experiences with hunting dogs don't necessarily come courtesy of established champions.

Over the years, I've raised and trained several competent, hard-working Labs but only one great one. And despite my own ability—shared by all but the most demanding retriever enthusiasts—to find admirable qualities in all those journeymen, I have to admit that the decade I hunted with the best felt qualitatively different from the rest of my waterfowling career. I hunted for Sky more than for myself and I regarded every hunt primarily as an opportunity to watch him amaze me. Now all that seems impossibly long ago, before I was married to Lori or had children of my own. But Lab people define their life passages by their dogs, and even though I wouldn't trade places with anyone as I enter my fifth decade of duck hunting, I'd trade anything—almost—to be able to hunt with Sky one more time.

With the single blue-wing resting between us on the bench, the dog and I turned our attention back toward the evening sky. My contemplative mood had not survived the appearance of the teal. The bird I killed over the decoys reminded me how much I loved to shoot ducks, while my futile second shot left me twitchy and eager to redeem myself the next time around. After all, no batter likes to end the game on a strikeout. Besides, the single dead blue-wing obligated me to pluck and clean without providing enough substance for a meal. The thought of even one more bird promised closure, and as the shadows began to creep across the marsh from the west, I did my best to conjure game from the still air overhead.

In contrast to the moth-winged teal, the next opportunity announced its arrival to the ear rather than the eye. Somewhere overhead a great tearing sound rent the air, but as I peered upward from the sheltering brim of my hat the sky remained stubbornly empty. As the noise rose to an improbable crescendo, I braced myself for the arrival of ducks in waves, a reasonable expectation that explains my surprise when the source of the disturbance finally declared itself. Flaps extended like a Super Cub dropping into a tight mountain strip, a single mallard appeared out of the darkest quadrant of the sky, plummeting toward the decoys at a dizzying rate of descent. Even now it's hard to imagine all that noise arising from a lone set of wings.

Honest shooting light was failing fast, but I could still easily identify the sharp demarcation between dark thorax and light underbelly that marked the bird as a drake, and as he slid by high overhead I rose to take him. The bird shuddered as the sound of the shot spilled across the lonely marsh, but I realized at once that I hadn't killed him outright.

Pivoting awkwardly, I tried to pick him up with the second barrel, but his momentum had already carried him out of range, leaving me with nothing to do but mark his course as he fluttered down toward the cattails.

Intensely irritated by my shooting, I broke the gun and removed the live shell from the second barrel. Instead of ending the evening with a touch of class, I now faced the disturbing prospect of a lost bird. The retrieve would have been a challenge for an experienced dog under ideal conditions, and with daylight fading I considered cutting my losses and heading for home on the spot. But Sky looked eager, and motivated more by a sense of obligation than any expectation of success, I gave him the line and sent him over the top of the blind.

As the dog surged away in the direction of the fall, I left the empty shotgun behind on the bench and waded out toward the decoys. Sunset had brought a flurry of activity to the sky over the distant edges of the marsh, but I didn't have any more shooting left in me. Besides, I reasoned, if the dog was willing to give the retrieve his undivided attention, I owed him a certain measure of courtesy in return. And so I ignored the birds in the air overhead and stood unarmed in the decoy spread, idly gathering up blocks and following the progress of the retrieve with my ears. Given the thickness of the cover where the wounded drake had fallen, I knew there was nothing I could do to advance the cause. The bird had become the dog's to find or to lose.

Sky sounded like a water buffalo as he worked his way through the brittle reeds. At first he seemed to cast about methodically, but then I heard him hesitate, and the sound of cattails breaking yielded to the wet gurgle of a diving dog. Point and counterpoint, these two noises receded deeper and deeper into the depths of the cover, leaving me with the mental image of a wily bird trying to capitalize on a young dog's lack of experience. But Sky refused to abandon the chase, and as I worked my way through the process of gathering the decoys, the sound of pursuit faded slowly from the range of my hearing.

By the time I returned to the blind for the gun and the teal and started around the edge of the water with the decoy bag over my shoulder, the long day had faded to nothing but a dull brassy glow above the western horizon. Suddenly the cattails parted and a widening wake appeared on the polished surface of the water with its apex pointed in my direction. Relieved by the dog's reappearance, I didn't even realize what he had done until he bounded from the water and presented the mallard, which I accepted in a state of near disbelief. The warm, sleek feel of its plumage and the heft of the bird in my hand felt like some kind of miracle.

And just the first of many, as subsequent seasons proved. But spectacular canine performances have a unique way of liberating the observer from the urge to look forward in time to events that may or may not take place. Beyond any measure of ducks lost or recovered, good dogs ground us firmly in the present, the best of all possible times for hunters and dogs alike. And it is just that sense of immediacy that I remember as I walked out of the marsh with a duck dinner in the game vest and the dog trailing along at my side. Together we had made something out of nothing. The rest could wait.

JAKE

by Dan O'Brien

Since my wife and I have been together, there have been several dogs in our household and Kris has loved them all. When we first met, her attraction for dogs was indiscriminate, embracing schizophrenic Pomeranians as passionately as finely focused English pointers. This, I felt sure, had to do with the fact that she had never seen a dog doing what a dog does best, hunting. I'd like to think it was my influence that created in Kris an understanding and love for hunting dogs, what they do, and how they can enrich your life. But, in fact, I was only a minor player in Kris's discovery. The real credit goes to Jake, who knew her long before I was on the scene.

You see, Kris was raised in southern California. She'd never been hunting, never fired a gun, and never seen a well-trained dog locate, point, or retrieve a bird. But despite this disadvantage, she was naturally drawn to dogs. One of the first things that attracted me to her was the eighty-pound black Lab–golden retriever cross that had been her companion through four years of medical school. One of the first serious things she ever said to me was that she wouldn't have made it through school if it hadn't been for Jake.

He was with her the whole way, bounced around from city to city, keeping her company when she was studying, and sometimes waiting inside sixteen hours at a stretch until she could get home to walk him. She went to school at Dartmouth and told me that some nights, when she got home, the combination of long hours and subzero temperatures conspired to depress her to the point of tears. But Jake was always there to greet her, and they walked every night and that's what gave her the strength to get up the next morning and do it again. The fact that she had learned the restorative powers of a relationship with a dog made me know she was special. And the fact that Jake had been the one to teach her made him special too. They got me thinking that my dream of finding a woman who would enjoy life afield with me and a dog might not be completely farfetched.

ॐ

Jake got his looks from his Lab side. Except for slightly longer hair, you'd have never known he wasn't pure Lab. He was one of those blocky dogs with a head like chiseled granite and had that gentle way of looking at you—like he felt vaguely sorry for you, being human and all. Like so many of the really good dogs, Jake seemed to know how he could best support the people with whom he lived. After Kris moved on to her internship and residency, where she had even less time, and I started hanging around, Jake shifted a portion of his allegiance to me. I'm sure he knew it was what Kris wanted and I was grateful to be included.

Kris was doing a two-year residency in Denver and I took to spending a lot of time there. I was used to sleeping alone and while sharing a bed with Kris was a welcome change, sharing a bed with Kris and Jake was not exactly what I had in mind. I remember coming face to face with Jake one of those first nights, when I pulled the covers back to get into bed, and thinking that I should throw him out. But he stared at me unflinchingly and I realized that this was not my call. I was the interloper here and was infringing on the unity of a serious, well-functioning team. I never saw anyone work as hard as Kris. Except for Jake, she had been alone in a seven-year battle to make something special of her life. Jake stayed on the bed.

I tried to understand what they had both been through. I found that Kris was gone a great deal, fourteen-hour days and on all-night call every third night. Jake and I were thrown together and it was good for both of us. Her house was on a busy street. The traffic was confining—something I was not used to. For good reason, Jake had seldom been off a leash and I seized this deprivation as an excuse for us to escape the city.

We began going on extended walks in more remote places than Jake was used to. Kris was a little more protective of him—suggesting that he wouldn't eat dog food without cooking oil and that November water was too cold for him to retrieve sticks from. She made it sound a little like Jake preferred tofu to T-bones, but after I started taking him to my home on a South Dakota ranch, inhabited by a new English setter puppy named Idaho Spud and an ancient basset hound named Morgan, I came to know something for sure about Jake that I had suspected all along.

Morgan had run rabbits every day since his retirement several years before. He was like an old demented pensioner returning to the office out of habit. He got up early, had a little drink of water, and usually struck a trail about seven thirty. He'd run rabbits until the heat of the day. Then he'd come into the barn for another drink and snooze until four o'clock when he'd go back at it for another couple hours. A little after dark he'd come in to eat and sleep, and it would start all over again about seven the next morning. He was slow and inefficient. But he took his work seriously and didn't pay much attention to this big, black city dog who stayed in the house. But I noticed that Jake watched Morgan from the kitchen window. I caught him several times studying the old-timer as he snooped through the grown-over farm equipment, and it wasn't long before the big head stiffened and the black ears came up at the sound of Morgan's strike.

Jake was aloof when it came to my hunting dogs, but he couldn't help keeping an eye on Spud as we went through yard training and limited recall quail work. This whole scene, with its cacophony of new smells, made him a little nervous and he disdained close contact with these dogs. But he was interested. When Kris came out to the ranch and made a fuss over these two ruffians, it threw Jake into a tail-spin. It was about that time that Kris began to take an interest herself. In me, I suppose, but more in the elements of my life. She asked about the roading harness, the electronic collar, and the dog boxes in the back of the pickup. She inspected the kennel, and though I knew she had a hard time understanding the reasoning behind this way of keeping dogs, she never made any judgments. She had seen Spud pointing a wing and was fascinated by the way this little moron puppy went so deadly serious over a game. She watched steady old Morgan going about his chores and began to see how important all this was to me.

After about the third visit she wondered if, the next time we went to the ranch, she couldn't try shooting a shotgun and I, of course, bent over backwards to comply. I planned to let her shoot my side-by-side twenty but my hired hand and comrade of twenty years shook his head. "That's a mistake," he said. "She won't hit anything and that little thing will kick her silly." When Kris arrived at the ranch for her first shoot-ing lesson, we had a brand-new Remington 1100 12-gauge with a shortened stock and butt pad waiting for her. She broke the first three clay pigeons she ever saw.

But, before there was any shooting, we had to put Jake in the basement. Though he had never seen a gun before, he was shy of explosions. Apparently, Fourth of July fireworks had rattled him. Kris told me every year he spent most of the Fourth trying to get under the refrigerator. I had a hard time believing it. With little Spud pistoning in his kennel and poor old blind Morgan limping out to investigate every dead clay pigeon, it was hard to imagine that a dog like Jake wouldn't be clambering to get in on the fun. But he sure wasn't.

Kris and I came into the house full of good thoughts about the possibility of Kris going pheasant hunting. The season was half over by then but there might be a good way to do some late-season hunting. She was delighted with the shotgun and the shooting. I was delighted that she was delighted. She even mentioned the idea that Jake might go with us on the pheasant hunt. I knew that notion made sense to her but I tried to gently discourage it. I restated my theo-ry that housedogs don't make good bird dogs and bird dogs don't make good housedogs. She looked at me oddly and said simply that I underestimated dogs. I know now she spoke from a native understanding, but then, I suppose, I only smiled.

When we went down into the basement, we found Jake quaking in a corner. It was a terrible sight and Kris was upset, so I didn't say anything like "I told you so." When she put her arms around him and apologized for shooting, I knew the plans for a pheasant hunt were in jeopardy. I felt my dream of having a woman to share my days in the field slipping away. But it was a dream worth dreaming and—theories be damned—I made myself a promise to fight for it.

Thank God, Jake loved cheese more than he feared anything.

Kris was skeptical, but after Jake figured that the sound of the cap gun wrapped in a towel meant cheddar, it wasn't long until the towel was discarded. Another week and you didn't want to be between him and the kitchen when the starter's pistol went off. Finally he'd come full bore across any field for a 12-gauge—and a quarter pound of gouda.

So I figured we at least had a chance. Dog over his gun shyness, new shotgun, first-time hunter, this had the potential to be fun. Kris was very excited about the possibility of bagging a few pheasants. She had recipes she wanted to try, and the idea of Jake becoming a focused bird dog, though I downplayed it, thrilled her.

But there was another catch. On a picnic, during a rare medical school break, when Jake was just a puppy, he had wandered off and been caught in a chicken coop, knee deep in fresh-plucked chickens. Kris said it was the first time he had ever seen birds up close but the owner was not in a forgiving mood and whacked Jake across the nose. "He hasn't shown much interest in birds since," Kris said.

She swore the punishment had only been one crisp thump across the muzzle so I assured her that there was no problem. Jake didn't mind gunfire now and he loved to retrieve. His natural instincts would take over and he'd do fine. That's what I told her. But I'd gotten to know Jake pretty well by then and knew he learned lessons for keeps. I was worried that his desire to do what people wanted him to do might very well extend to that New Hampshire farmer. In an attempt to avoid a bad day in the field, when we did finally take Jake out, I dug a Hungarian partridge out of the freezer —partridge caddis can be a hot trout fly in the Black Hills — and thawed it one morning when Kris was at work. That afternoon I went into the backyard where Jake and I normally played fetch with tennis balls and sticks.

He leaped and twisted with joy when I held the stick over his head but sat, trembling with anticipation, when I gave the command. I threw the stick twice, and he pounded after it, delivering it to hand when I asked. The third time I surreptitiously substituted the partridge from my pocket for the stick and sent him off after it with an encouraging "fetch." He bore down on it like a goshawk but never laid a tooth on it. As soon as he recognized it as a bird he pulled up like it was cow pie and trotted quickly back to my side. He looked up at me like I'd pulled the dirtiest trick in the book, and I knew I had a problem.

By this time, Kris was counting on a pheasant hunt so I reassured Jake by putting my arm around him. But that didn't help much. The nervous look in his eye told me that I'd better quickly get him back into retrieving or I'd have an even bigger problem on my hands. I went back to the house for his favorite toy—a green Day-Glo Frisbee—and this snapped him out of his paranoia. He did the happy dog dance complete with leaps and yips and I sailed the Frisbee out for him to chase. He was a pro—a veteran of San Diego beaches and Ivy League campuses—and made a long graceful lunge, picking the Frisbee neatly out of midair. It dawned on me that this might be the key.

I found a roll of duct tape under the seat of my pickup and, out of Jake's sight, taped the partridge to the top of the Frisbee. Then, in my most affected, excited voice, I encouraged Jake in his own excitement. I held the Frisbee above him—with the partridge safely on top and out of sight—and he leaped and yipped. And when I sent it wobbling out into the yard he charged after it as usual. But when he came close, he jumped back like he'd found a rattlesnake. Still, he knew the Frisbee was there and wanted badly to bring it back. He didn't return to my side but sat down looking at the problem. Finally he reached out and, with his lips curled delicately back, took the very edge of the Frisbee in his teeth and drug the whole works back to lie at my feet. Never did he, in any way, come in contact with a feather.

We had to start with a single tail feather taped to the Frisbee and work up through two feathers, one wing, two wings, and eventually a whole bird. But in a week, he was over his dread of dead birds. It took another two weeks and a very tolerant pigeon to get him to put a moving feathered object into his mouth. But once he caught on, he was a natural. In no time, he was making seventy-five-yard blind retrieves and doing it with extreme enthusiasm.

While all this was going on, I was working with Spud, getting him ready for his first exposure to pheasants. I didn't expect much from such a pup but figured him to put a few birds up. I ran the two dogs together on a route that included several stock dams and, of course, Jake would dive headlong into each dam as we came to it. If it was a hot day, he'd swim around for five or ten minutes and Spud, who was still only a year old, got so he'd follow Jake right on in. To this day, Spud is the swimmingest setter I've ever seen and I attribute that to Jake.

In a lot of ways, Jake was Spud's hero during that first summer and fall of life, but I wondered what Spud would think of his idol if he failed to retrieve a shot bird or, worse yet, just stuck close to Kris and didn't hunt. Spud has always been a go-getting dog and I had no worries that he wouldn't hunt hard. His problem, if anything, would be overzealousness, and that is a good kind of problem to have. Jake, on the other hand, might decide he didn't go for this rowdy life and quit. I was afraid that he might influence Kris to do the same.

In the days before our pheasant hunt, I got worried that Jake and Kris would have a bad day. Experienced hunters know that bad days happen and that you should just forget them. If the dog screws up or you can't shoot well, put it behind you—things will be better next time. But a bad day could be fatal for a thirty-year-old with high expectations of hunting with her faithful old housedog—both for the first time. And I didn't want Kris's interest to die. I knew that if it did, my life would veer from its ideal path, and I'd find myself hunting mostly solo.

So the importance of the pheasant hunt began to take on cosmic proportions, and by the time the day arrived I was a worried wreck, and Jake must have been getting tired of retrieving that same duct-taped pigeon—with one wing left loose to flap. I had done everything I could but still I was not confident. I worried about Jake drawing a tough old rooster with only a broken wing for his first retrieve, I worried about

Kris's shooting, and I worried that I wouldn't be able to resist kibitzing.

By the time everything was ready it was late in the season and the wild birds had been worked over pretty hard. In an effort to control some of the variables, I chose a hunting preserve owned by a friend as the venue for our outing. Twenty dollars a bird seemed awfully high but my friend guaranteed there would be birds out there, and I reasoned that the team I was bringing—Kris, Jake, Spud, and myself— was not exactly a well-oiled hunting machine that could run up a huge bill.

The day dawned gray and overcast and low, flat clouds threatened rain. It was not the kind of day I'd hoped for, but the weather report was for clearing with a light, warm breeze. I offered up a little prayer to Orion as I loaded Spud into his dog box. Jake had had only a few lessons in kenneling into a dog box, but he loaded all right and we were on the road by eight o'clock.

Kris was nearing the end of her residency and we had begun to talk about what would happen the next year. There were big job opportunities in California, Chicago, about any big city, but she didn't want to go there. She had come to like South Dakota and thought she liked the kinds of things we were doing that day. I looked at the sky as we pulled into my friend's shooting reserve. There was a faint streak of blue directly overhead, but the horizons were still caulk, and snow was still not out of the question.

My friend pointed us down the road to a half section of thick brome grass and old weedy milo fields along the edge of standing corn. There was a marshy spot there too, and cattails grew thick below a large stock dam from which we could hear the sounds of geese and mallards. We unloaded near the standing corn but, when we started out, I pointed Spud in the other direction. I knew there would be birds in the corn, and if he got in there, all we'd see would be roosters spiraling up like distant missiles.

I carried a gun but wasn't out to shoot. I hoped Spud would find a few birds and maybe flash point one or two. What I was really there for was to see to it that Kris had a good time. But it started out poorly. A rooster jumped at her feet before we were thirty yards from the truck and she fired twice before the stock had even touched her shoulder. She probably fired fifteen feet over the bird. Jake didn't flinch at the shots but didn't pay much attention to the bird either. Spud chased it out of sight.

While we waited for the little imp to return—which he did in fifteen minutes with his tongue nearly dragging—I tried to keep Kris's mood light. She's a competitive person and was used to breaking clay pigeons. She was instantly mad at herself for missing—the beginner's mistake—and I was afraid it would affect her whole day. I seldom care if a bird comes to bag, but that day it seemed crucial. I laughed it off, "Everybody misses, forget it. Take your time. You got lots of time." And the more I talked the more I knew it was the wrong thing to do. I had to force myself to shut up. We waited in silence and Jake lay down at Kris's feet. When Spud finally returned, Jake got up and sniffed the huffing Spud as if to ask what the big deal was.

We set off again, walking along the edge of the cattails, and the sky began to clear. The winter browns went rich with shadow and we both praised the changing weather. Suddenly it was pleasant just walking there with Kris. This was more like my dream. Spud was somewhere in the next county but I wasn't going to let that spoil the day. Jake had begun to potter ahead of us, and it was possible he might stumble onto a pheasant. Kris and I were both beginning to stop trying so hard and enjoy the day when Spud angled in from somewhere and flushed a pheasant twenty-five yards to our left.

I didn't even pull up on it. It was out a good ways and one of those tough crossing shots. But Kris brought her gun up and poked a shot at it. I winced when I saw the gun barrel stop just before she shot. The bird was going forty miles an hour by then. She missed it by a mile. "You got to keep the gun moving," I said before I thought to say it diplomatically.

Kris frowned. "I don't know about this," she said. It was in the tone of voice I had dreaded for weeks and I felt a touch of panic. It was me. I was making her crazy.

"Look," I said. "Spud is running amok. I'm going to take him up in that brome grass where I can keep an eye on him. You take Jake and walk up to the dam, then back through the cattails. There should be birds in the cattails for sure."

I gathered Spud up and headed out. I figured the only chance was to leave her alone and hope the improving weather would work its magic. As I started uphill toward the brome bench, I saw Jake watching me. He looked from me to Kris and back again. At the time, I thought he was just confused about our splitting up. But now, I think he had sensed the tension in the air. I believe he was evaluating things—trying to understand what was at stake.

❧

The day won me over. As soon as I started to concentrate on Spud, everything mellowed. He was wearing me down, and I stayed on him until he was quartering in front of me fairly well. We worked up through the brome for a quarter mile and he bumped a pheasant. I whoaed him and got in to where I could praise him. After we made the turn and started back, he hit another one and held it until I was in range. When it came up, I shot and killed Spud's first bird.

We celebrated with a good petting in the dry grass, and for an instant I forgot about Kris and Jake. But when we got walking again, there was still a nagging feeling in the back of my head, and when we came to where we could look down on the cattail slough I was holding my breath, hoping Kris and Jake were not back at the pickup.

They were still hunting the cattails and I resisted going down to join them. Spud and I sat down in the golden grass above them and watched. They didn't really know where to look for birds and they wandered to areas that seldom hold them. It was all I could do not to shout directions from my hill. But Jake was out front and quartering within range and they looked happy enough. I had Spud on a lead and we settled in to enjoy watching the woman I loved work her first cattail slough with her pet retriever. I was afraid it would look like Abbott and Costello on a hunt. But they didn't look too bad. Their demeanor had changed since I'd last seen them. They were concentrating on what they were doing yet casual and relaxed. Something magical had happened in my absence and I saw an ease in Kris's walk that I'd never seen before, but have seen a thousand times since.

They were certainly pushing birds in front of them and, the way they were working the slough, they might just run into a herd of them at the end where they'd have to fly or run across a dirt road. There was a particular corner of firebush that looked great and Jake was leading Kris right to it.

I sat up a little as they approached the firebush. It looked like Jake's gait picked up. His tail was ringing! He began to bounce and up came a bird. Bang—and it folded. I couldn't believe it. It was beautiful. Jake charged into the brush and brought the bird to Kris. I could hear her squeal with delight.

But Jake just spit it into her hand and dove back into the bush. Up came another pheasant. Bang. Another perfect retrieve. Back into the bushes. Two birds. Bang, bang! and Kris stopped to reload while Jake searched out the birds.

Then birds were coming up everywhere. Bang! Bang! Kris had two more down before the rocketing pheasants turned into twenty-dollar bills in my mind. I struggled to my feet. "Wait." But Jake was still working the brush and I hustled toward them with Spud straining at the leash.

When I got there, Kris had six birds lined up at her feet. The gun was empty and she was kneeling with her arms around a panting, very happy retriever. She beamed up at me and I beamed back.

For weeks afterward, all she could talk about was how great the hunt had been. Winter set in with a vengeance then and we didn't get a chance to go hunting again that year. But she was hooked deep. We lived off that day for months and it became part of our history, part of what makes us what we are.

Old Morgan died not long after and, though you always take the death of a good dog hard, we knew it was his time and he'd lived a full life. The real shock came early that spring, just after Kris and I decided to make our desire to spend the rest of our lives together official. It was the spring of Kris's last year of residency and we planned to get married and live in South Dakota where the whole bunch of us could enjoy a little more freedom than most people are used to.

Jake had not seemed his old self for a couple days and we took him to the vet's for a checkup. The vet wanted to keep him overnight for some tests and we really didn't think too much of it. But early in the morning—it was a Sunday because Kris was home—he called to say that Jake had died. Kris was speechless and handed the phone to me.

I listened dumbfounded while this perfectly nice young vet tried to explain. He was terribly upset and obviously had no idea what had really happened. I listened to him rattle on, searching for the explanation he never found. The cause of death was unknown. But I knew why Jake was dead. It all fell into place for me that morning and the knowledge changed my life.

Jake died because his job was done. He'd seen Kris through medical school, her internship, and her residency— been there through some rough and lonely times. He'd brought her from a college girl to a woman aware of so much more. He led her through important stages of her life, and he led her through that cattail slough and into that flock of pheasants. He'd eased her gently into a new, more vital life and he was counting on me to take it from there.

It was a terribly sad time in our lives and most of the day I held Kris, and rocked her, and tried my best to make her see what Jake had given her. But his gifts were not only for Kris. I've come to know that he gave a great deal to me too. He made a dream come true.

Now Kris and I gun for pheasant, and grouse and woodcock and quail and partridge. We do it with joy and reverence. And we do it with good birds dogs that live like Jake always did. Idaho Spud is older now and has been joined by Old Hemlock Melville, who is learning the trade and promises to carry on a tradition. They both live in the house. They sleep on our bed with us, and some nights, when Spud is hard beside me and Mel is pressing against Kris and they are both rolling the blanket under them and shrink-wrapping Kris and me closer and closer, I think this is the way Jake wanted it all along. His big square head with the deep, dark eyes floats through my dreams. His wisdom haunts me.

HONEY AND CLYDE

by John Hewitt

I t would not be overstating the case to say that Labrador retrievers are taking over the world. I know several people who own two. Come to think of it, I do myself. But this was not always the case. Especially in Topeka in the 1940s and '50s.

As a youngster, I classified Labs somewhere between California condors and ivory-billed woodpeckers: some old-timers may have seen one once, a long time ago, but I certainly had not. So when a black one ambled out of a yard halfway between Joyce Meyer's house and Sumner Elementary when I was nine and already late for school, I ran all the way home to tell my mother.

The only person I knew who'd actually seen one and even hunted with it was Ted Zercher, in the 1930s, up on the Platte River in Nebraska. There was a snapshot in a shoe box in his closet of him holding his pump shotgun and two Canadas. The Lab is absent. But many times I heard the story of the retrieve of his second goose, barely wing-broken and swimming strongly in a December river running ice. The dog and the goose both headed around a downstream bend, almost out of sight, and the dog returned with the goose in his mouth, still alive, a half hour later.

The never-asked-or-answered question this story raised every time I heard it was why didn't we have one? Probably because Ted and Clyde, my grandfather and father, respectively, had only hunted ducks seriously since 1934 and both already had bird dogs for quail. And the Great Depression was lingering on. About the time both Ted's wife and her Airedale died, leaving him with a nine-year-old daughter, he decided that what the girl needed was a dog, and bought Mary Liz a small cocker spaniel puppy, a bitch that, due to its coloration, she named "Honey."

Except during November, the pointers lived out their incarceration in a scabbed-together kennel with a six-foot fence and a four-foot extension on top. On top of the extension, insulators and one strand of galvanized wire hooked to a transformer, putting out enough voltage to bring a Hereford to its knees. Or knock me off a six-foot stepladder when I touched it with a coffee can. Or knock my twin brother off the same ladder as soon as I talked him into trying it.

Honey, unlike the pointers, had the run of the place, and spent her summers in a deep hole she'd dug in the shade under the porch. This was before air-conditioning, and I can say, after much testing, that hers was the coolest spot on the property, especially with a little breeze.

No hunting dog ever set out afield with less formal education than Honey. She would come when called, at least at suppertime, and bring back a thrown tennis ball, if it was not too hot out. This was at the close of an era when a cocker, no less than a springer or the Brittany no one had even heard of yet, was considered to be a legitimate hunting dog.

Since Ted took Mary Liz duck hunting as often as she wanted, and even bought her a Winchester .410 pump, Honey got to go also. Once the cocker learned that after the crouching, whispering, duck calling, and shooting there was usually something a lot more elemental than a tennis ball to retrieve, the men decided they might as well have left the decoys at home.

The two of them wore hip boots and could retrieve many of the ducks themselves, as they continued to do when several were knocked down. But the Kansas River had a current, and a channel, and sometimes the water level rose. But for the little cocker, quite a few birds every fall would have been lost.

Honey's main drawback was that she was no taller than a rat terrier or a beagle. A floating or swimming duck at any great distance from the sandbar was very difficult for her to see. Clyde's solution to this problem was to set his shotgun down, hoist Honey above his head in both hands, and point her in the direction of the duck, while striding downstream to stay abreast of it. Upon spotting it, she'd whine and wriggle violently, he'd lower her to the ground, and she'd scamper into the water up to her chin and swim, eyes still on the duck. What this method lacked in style points, it made up for in effectiveness.

Once Honey got the duck in her mouth, she hadn't the strength to push against the current, so the method required someone to keep pace with her on the bank as she was carried downstream, and keep her pointing across the current as she finished the retrieve. If she ever got pointed straight upstream, she began losing ground and got farther and farther away. We did not want to find out what would happen if she were left out there fighting the current for too long.

My twin, Tom, and I got to go along for the first time on a warm and duckless October day when we were about four and our mother could drive us to the river in the broad daylight, where we met the hunters who'd been out since before sunrise. Once there, we took Honey for a walk and fed her the ends of our hot dogs, roasted on willow sticks over a driftwood fire, and wrapped up decoy anchor cords when the men waded out and brought them ashore. There were flocks of killdeers and several crows, four or five kinds of hawks that Ted identified for us, a high flock or two of ducks, water-smoothed pieces of flint edging the bar, and a host of oddly shaped, gray pieces of driftwood and other treasures buried in the huge drift piles.

Thereafter, we lobbied incessantly for more duck hunts, and by the time we were seven and got BB guns, we began having some success. We even got them to get us up early and make the drive in the dark, never mind that the car ride always put us to sleep again.

The year Honey was fifteen we had some rain in November and the river began rising at midweek. By Saturday morning the newspaper said it was up two feet, and there was a little worry about the blind being in the water. After the drive it was almost a half-mile hike down a bare fence line to the woods, through the woods in the moonlight, then out on the sandbar. Clyde and Ted carried double sacks of mallard decoys, while Tom and I had a single sack each, half full. The men also carried their shotguns, Winchester pumps in 12- and 20-gauge, in padded canvas cases over their shoulders.

"Well, Ted," Clyde said from up ahead, "at least we didn't lose the blind." In fact, its location had probably improved, as the decoy water now included a shallow backwater a few inches deep behind the blind, where I put all the decoys from my sack. Honey waded gingerly out to the blind and hopped in over the lowest end log. By the time the decoys were all out, it was getting fairly light in the east, prompting Clyde to haul out the gold Hamilton pocket watch that his father had given him on the same birthday as the shotgun. "By the time we get loaded up, it'll be about shooting time," he said.

Pushing a red-paper-hulled Winchester No. 6 into his magazine, Clyde said, "As deep as it is just beyond the decoys, we don't want Honey getting after any swimming cripples. The river's got too big on us and we could lose her." We sat in silence a few minutes while the several coveys of quail within hearing tuned up.

"And don't forget what we always say: If you don't see two or three bunches before shooting time on the river, it's not going to be much of a day," Clyde added. We had seen none.

As the sun was just showing red through the bare downstream cottonwoods, a half dozen specks appeared upriver—low and pretty interesting. Ted blew a hail call on his black P. S. Olt duck call and quit when they banked our way.

"Oh-oh, Clyde," Ted warned. "Better hold off on these. They look a lot like…"

"Wood ducks," Clyde said. Due to low population numbers, neither wood ducks nor prairie chickens were legal then. "Go ahead and take a good look at this bunch, boys." We poked our heads out of the top of the blind, which was not allowed ordinarily when ducks were circling. Our job was to remain curled up on the floor, throttling the dog, though we could peek out between bottom logs if we could find a spot. The wood ducks, four of which were drakes, banked over the decoys and continued on downriver.

"Well, that was encouraging," Ted said. "Now we know the layout doesn't look too bad. At least to wood ducks."

An even smaller bunch of teal, greenwings probably, passed low to the water a half hour later—two hundred yards away across the rising river—and ignored both duck calls.

It was midmorning before we saw a mallard. Two dozen came out from behind a stand of cottonwoods upstream and across. They were a mile away, low and very decoyable, and from the look of it, had probably just come from a riverbottom cornfield. At the distance of a quarter mile, with the first quack on the calls, they set their wings, made one wide circle, and came straight in—rocking back and forth on cupped wings.

"Take 'em!" Ted said. Since he was oldest and shot the 20-gauge, he usually called the shot. The men stood up, the mallards flared, and we let Honey go. Pungent-smelling empties rained down around us as we peeked out, and the shooting was over only two or three heartbeats after it began.

One drake in the decoys on his back, flopping one wing, caught Honey's eye, and in she went. Clyde made it as far as the edge of the water before he reached into a canvas hunting coat pocket, pulled out another No. 6, dropped it in his 12-gauge, and laid a pattern of shot across the only cripple, a hen below and beyond the decoys. She, too, rolled over and kicked one foot in the air.

Ted reached a drake he had shot at the upper edge of the decoy set without going in above his knees, and Clyde got two more from below. Tom and I took Honey's drake from her as soon as she was back into water shallow enough for our four-buckle galoshes, and we ran downstream with her toward Clyde, who was keeping pace with the hen.

"Here, boys," he said, and handed me his 12-gauge. I took it and he picked the wet dog up, heaved her up over his head, and continued south, while she dripped all over him. In only a few steps, the wiggling and whining began.

"She sees 'im! She sees 'im!" we chorused. Clyde set her down and she plunged in.

Although only a gun range out, for a dog Honey's size it was a long retrieve, and not many duck dogs her age even get taken afield. Before the water had risen, there had been a narrow channel, not more than knee deep, which cut diagonally through our sandbar some two hundred yards below the blind. It was deeper and much wider now, not crossable by a man in only hip boots, especially a man as short as Clyde. I was young, but not too young to experience a cold fear growing somewhere inside. I had thought that fatal disasters must happen in an instant, but this one was unfolding at a walking pace, the speed of the current.

By the time Honey had reached the duck, grabbed it, and turned shoreward, Clyde was shaking his head as he walked. "Never make it," he said. Tom and I, with Honey's first duck and Clyde's gun, were right at his heels. When Clyde reached the edge of the channel, he handed us a drake apiece; picked up a stout, limbless length of driftwood for a wading staff; and waded in. He was almost up to the top of his boots when Ted joined us at the lowest tip of our bar. We laid the four mallards in a row on the sand and watched the dog struggling toward Clyde.

"C'mon, girl. C'mon!" he said, at the limit of his boots. When he had to stop, Honey was forty feet out, and the farther down she got, the more she came around to face the current, trying to reach him. In less than a minute, she was swimming straight upstream, or trying to. She held her own for a few moments, and then the mallard in her mouth began getting farther away, because that was all we could see. Clyde jabbed the staff into the riverbottom downstream of him, gripped firmly with both hands, and took a couple of tentative steps.

"Let her go, Clyde!" Ted shouted. "Just let her go!"

In the roster of dangers of childhood, Tom and I had been taught—from the time we could crawl—to be afraid of three things: the butcher knife in the kitchen drawer, the shotguns behind the dining room door, and the river. Eventually, we would learn to handle all three safely, but Ted had lost a brother to a shotgun and our mother had lost two cousins to the river. At nine, we were still steering clear of all these things. We had no doubts about what happened to people who got into a river that was too deep.

Clyde did not pause again, and the water lapped at the hem of his hunting coat, then at the waist.

"Well," Ted said, "that's the end of his good pocket watch..."

When Clyde was in water up to his armpits, the current was moving him downstream in spite of his staff, since his buoyancy was trying to lift his feet from the bottom. He half-stumbled on something on the bottom, caught himself, and began emerging from the river, step by step, as the bottom sloped upward to the other bank.

Once safely on the lower bar, Clyde lay on his back and stuck his feet into the air to drain his boots. Then he got back up and trotted downstream to get Honey pointed toward shore again.

By the time the tiny figures of man and dog finally met and seemed to touch as he took the duck, they were over a quarter mile distant. Tom and I cheered, but Clyde probably could not hear us. Ted just shook his head and smiled.

When they got to the edge of the channel on the way back, Clyde picked up the staff with one hand and enfolded the cocker and duck with his other arm—like a wet, furry football. This time he let the current take him more downstream, not fighting it as before, and the water rose right up over his hip boots again.

"Your dad," Ted said, "was too young for the first war and too old for the last one, but you have to think he'd have made a good soldier."

GRAY MUZZLES

by John R. Wright

For the fourth time since turning in, I raise up to check the glowing clock face. It is finally 4 A.M. and time to roll out. I swing my legs over the edge of the bed and the dog hears the springs complain. She pulls herself up with effort. She's wanted one of those L. L. Bean cedar dog beds for years, but the old couch cushion with a quilt over it seems to satisfy.

She passes me on the stairs as we go down, our joints all a-pop. Neither of our bladders is what it used to be, so she is as happy to be let out as I am to get to the bathroom. By the time I have the coffee started, she asks to come back in.

We're going out for ducks today, like so many times before. I've been a hunter for more than thirty years. She was born one. She'll be nine her next birthday, and I'll be forty-six.

Peach, named for the shade of her yellow Lab's coat, goes back upstairs for a few more winks before we head out. The dekes are already in the truck and the ancient, patched waders hang warming by the woodstove. Things were checked through and laid out last night, so I need little time to locate calls, whistle, shells, and fowling piece. But it does take a while, at that.

The squashed disk in my neck is making itself known this morning, sending waves of dull pain down my right shoulder and arm. The recoil of magnum duck loads won't go unnoticed today. Then there are the less insistent naggings, from knees, elbows, and other parts, all eager to remind me that football does, indeed, build character. Peach in not without her miseries, either. She seems to be a touch arthritic this season, packing her right rear leg at times, sitting with it shot out straight, and generally trying to keep her weight off it.

The coffee's ready and after an eye-opening, scalding slug, I return to the bathroom and the medicine cabinet to fetch an aspirin for the dog. She patiently accepts her pill by way of my finger poked down her throat.

I start the truck, then come back in to finish the coffee. My back is starting to loosen up and by now I can bend over enough to duct-tape my socks to my pant legs. If I fail to do this, the socks will be wadded into the toes of my wader boots before I've gone fifty feet. Peach hears the truck running and comes back downstairs. She, too, is moving a little easier and reminds me that's she's ready for breakfast.

Outside, I drop the tailgate and open the door of her dog box. She waits politely for the command "Load up." Her jump is good, but for that bad leg, which trails a bit behind. I'm standing by and give her just a little push—she would have made it anyway. In the cab I run my checklist once more. Decoys, calls, whistle, license, half a box of steel No. 1s, and the old double.

Ten minutes from home is the all-night market where I stop to fill my go mug. Somehow, their coffee is always better than mine. I get a couple of doughnuts I hardly need and nuke them a little in the microwave. Hunter and dog are better larded this season than last. I draw a stare from the wormy-looking graveyard clerk. I guess it's the lanyard and calls around my neck. Them's my "bonafidees," I think to myself. Man's gotta have proof of a good reason to be out and about this early. Don't want to look like some drunk who hasn't gotten to bed yet.

Back at the truck, I push the last bit of doughnut through the grill of the dog box and watch it vanish. This produces a series of tail thumps against crate sides.

It's black as the inside of a bull when we get to the reservoir. I'm always early or late. The engine runs, the heater blows, and I drink more coffee, intimidated by the thought of setting out blocks in the waist-deep water. The small, persistent leak in the crouch of my waders remains unfound and so unrepaired. There's nothing but country on the radio at 5:45 A.M. and I finish the coffee as some unidentified downhome crooner laments his misspent youth. You and me both, Bubba.

The faintest dab of pink in the east spurs me to action. The dog jumps stiffly to the ground, but limbers up fast and is soon rolling on her back in the snow. While I heft decoys, bird vest, and gun, Peach rushes into the remaining blackness like the pup that still rules her heart. She checks back shortly before I reach the lake's edge and I heel her up to keep her out of the water. Her habit of swimming out with me as I set the decoys is too taxing for her these days. Better to spare that bone-wracking chill for honest retrieving.

One of the dekes has a massive fissure in its belly, so eleven will have to do. By then, I feel the magic fingers of ice water tickling at my nether regions and I'm very anxious to make landfall. My bird vest goes down in the cattails for the dog to sit on as I arrange spare shells and break off stalks that might impede my swing. No blind here, just the old "hunker down in the weeds" routine. Then I stand and wait for daylight. I have found that legal shooting time and enough illumination for the dog to mark usually arrive at about the same pace.

It's brightening fast now and I load up. The dog's ears rise at the snap of the closing action and again as I tune up on the call. No slowing of the blood here. Her anticipation is as strong now as in her first season. Mine too.

I'm cold, though, and it occurs to me that a certain amount of toughness has been lost over the years. Seldom anymore do I undertake the long, wet belly crawl to jump maybe one bird that was standard operating procedure a few seasons back. The great need to shoot the gun and fill the bag has drawn away some and simply being here takes on new dimensions. But for the dog to work, which has become everything for the both of us, the odd duck must be killed. As if summoned by that thought, a bluebill sizzles by at Mach-2 with me standing tall and flat-footed. Raising the gun from a very relaxed port arms I mount it, release the safety, socket the butt into that shooter's sweet spot, swing hard, and in one oily-smooth motion, shoot at least four feet behind the bird. Peach watches the duck, looking for a hitch or a wobble, but ultimately has no reason to leave her seat.

Birds are in the air now, and I kneel in the snowy cattails, recharge the right barrel, and send out a hail call to whom it may concern. My knees are soon a pair of burning pincushions, part from the cold and part from the reluctance to bend. So much has been left on the playing field. A glance at the dog tells me she feels it too, that suspect leg extended out from under her weight. And so it goes for the next hour. Another pass by. Another miss.

I am contemplating an organized retreat when that absolutely griping sound comes to us from above and behind—wind slicing through pinion feathers—and I hunch down and crane my neck to see two drakes with bottle-green heads drop and turn out past the far edge of the stool, coming about into the wind and across the gun at sixty yards. I wait and fight to stay still, my heart doing that trip-hammer jig it learned long ago. As the birds cup wings and toe up to that invisible dead-certain mark, I get an instantaneous and totally dominating cramp in my right hip causing me to lurch and come to my feet as if on strings. The birds flare at forty yards, towering rapidly and putting distance between us.

Then in a slow-motion reversal of fortune, things begin to work. The pain fades as the gun lifts itself and tracks the high bird, tracing its bead along the stretched green neck, going past and building daylight. Swinging harder still, I pull the back trigger for the choke barrel. The kick is not felt, the report not heard. But I see the drake tumble and the dog go, both casting up diamond slivers of skim ice as they hit the water together.

He's a cripple, leading the dog on a merry chase out beyond the ice rim. At seventy-five yards she finally dives with him, going under, head and all. When she gets back she's winded, but has the duck and delivers to hand.

As always, she is very proud of herself and well she should be. She has broken through ice and fought her way to clear sailing. She has gone round and round with a diving cripple and done what all dogs hate—gotten her ears full of ice water on her subsurface retrieve. She has done a smashing good job and she knows it, jumping straight up and down as I praise her, pet her, and admire the duck.

It's a nice fat bird and she wants to worry it a little. I sack it and rub her up with the decoy bag. She likes this and thanks me with "that look." By now the morning flight is over, so we elect to go home. Peach is happy, knowing that when she is wet and it's just the two of us, she gets to ride in the cab with me.

At the cabin again she gets another aspirin and I get the whiskey jug down. She curls up behind the woodstove as I toss in a chunk. Soon she is twitching in dreams I wish I could see. Her face has turned almost completely white now and, wiping my mustache, I realize mine has too. But the marsh was made for two gray muzzles like us. And you know what? After our nap, there's the evening flight.

THOR

by Jay Reed

I f I could look back over my life and select just one day and be able to make it last forever, I know which one it would be. Easy choice. A no-brainer, as they say.

It would be that late October day, deep in the swamps of the Chippewa River, the wind curling and snapping out of the northeast, the temperature dropping, when my old dog told me he was going to die soon.

Thor was in his twelfth year that fall. Already a living legend, arguably the best-known hunting dog in the Midwest, he displayed the wear and tear of the miles that had gone before. But his eyes were bright and his heart was strong and the desire that drove him through the stubble fields of Saskatchewan, to the prairies of South Dakota, to the flooded low country of Mexico, to every crook and corner of Wisconsin and Iowa and Nebraska still burned within.

The yellow Labrador had been the subject of countless newspaper and magazine stories over the years. He had hunted for, and with, some of the biggest names in the conservation field. And most of those people remember him to this day as the best duck dog they ever saw. But I knew it would be that way, or had a hunch, at least, when he was eight months old.

He weighed about seventy pounds then, and he had grown gangly, leggy. But his chest was deep and his back was straight and his flanks rippled with hardening muscle. And he loved to train. He was not only willing to make one more retrieve, go through one more exercise. He wanted to.

The proof of anything is in performance, right? At that young age, Thor demonstrated extraordinary ability before a hundred or so spectators at a dog-training seminar. He was flawless. He made two long, spectacular water retrieves through the toughest swamp cover, drawing applause from those who watched and easily out-hunting two other retrievers three times his age.

Back then, Thor's biggest problem was his inability to stand by and watch other retrievers work. He was over-eager. He wanted to make every retrieve. He wanted to do every exercise. He was not a "gentleman on line," as they said in field training. And, every so often, he tried to cheat on his retrieves. He'd stay off the line. But he could mark a downed bird like a champion. And he was steady to shot from the beginning.

And he learned. There were those who said that Thor should have been good. He had the blood for it. His sire, Candlewood's Nifty Nick, was a Wisconsin open-field-trial champion and one of the state's most celebrated stud dogs. Thor looked like Nifty Nick, hunted like him, behaved like him, and displayed many of the dog's most significant traits. I thought about all that, and more, that day in the Chippewa River marshes. I knew that Thor was getting on toward the end of the line, but I never allowed myself to think that he would one day die. And it remains painful for me to recall all of that, even now that the snows of two winters have fallen upon his grave. It hurts me to think about it, like having the same tooth filled three times in one day. So consider the recounting of it all here as a sort of therapy for an old man who still sees the ghost of his dog every day and in his troubled dreams at night.

Ꮬ

This is how it was that day in October when Thor told me he was about to die. We are at our hunting camp in west central Wisconsin, a place of paradise where laughter is paramount and tears are few.

There is happiness: An old dog courses the swamps and finds the fountain of youth there. He becomes, as he once

EIGHTEEN

was, a pup, and he works the water and the wind and the cover and the birds with style and grace and uncommon dignity.

And there is sadness: The old dog has been fed and he has slept and now it is morning and I have to lift him off the couch where he spent the night because his muscles have tightened and his feet are sore and he is old, with only heart and wanting left to pump the engine. The fountain of youth was false.

Or was it?

With each step after that, he loosens up, and when he sees me put the shotgun into the truck, his eyes glisten and his tail wags. He is ready. He wants to go. He will go. Which is why I want to cry, because I know my time is running out for the dog, and so the hot tears roll down my cheek on a frosty dawn when only the stars can see.

Then I lift him into the truck, an assist that his eyes and gentle growl tell me he does not want. But I do it, and he accepts it because we both know this is how it has to be. And then I drive to the hunting grounds, and the old dog tries to stand in the back of the truck, but he can't because his legs won't let him. So he sits, growling softly, his heart telling him that these are the good times, the best of times.

Maybe he knows his days are numbered. Maybe he knows that there are not that many more retrieves for him to make. Maybe he knows that for him, one day soon, the sunset will write a final chapter to this business called duck hunting, this business called life. Maybe he knows all of that. But I do not. Yet.

He jumps, unaided, to the ground when we reach the boat landing. He is loosening up now. When the boat is in the water, he steps into it without a problem, stationing himself, as he has done for a lifetime, close to the stern where I can scratch his ears as we travel into the swamps.

We run for an hour through some of the most beautiful marshland God ever created. Thor knows every inch of it. He has worked it all. He puts his nose into the wind and inhales it deeply. The wind is a river of language to the old dog. He reads it the way the rest of us read books. It is a blue domain, designed only for him.

We reach our pothole of choice. Shouldering the shotgun, a bag of decoys, and a pack with lunch, I lead the twenty-minute walk to the place where we have this little blind. There is a bucket for me to sit on. And there is a dry patch of canvas, plus a blanket, upon which Thor can either sit or stand out of the water while we wait for the ducks to come. And they do. But we are selective. There is no need to hurry. We have all day. So take only the best, I tell myself. Let it all last. Let it all linger.

But a mallard drake works the decoys. It swings once and then comes in, wings set. An artist should capture it. I pull on the bird, squeeze the trigger, and it drops into a combination stand of tall marsh grass and buck brush. Thor marks the spot and, on command, goes to fetch.

He works it exactly right and, finally, he emerges from the heavy cover holding the mallard in the classic breast grip. The dog comes straight to hand, duck held high out of the water. He comes to me, walks around to my side and sits, offering me the result of all we have worked for, all we have trained for, all we have bragged about and publicly demonstrated over the years. If there is such a thing in this world as a perfect retrieve, this was it.

I take the bird and pat the dog on his heaving sides and tell him that it was good work. He shakes himself, swamp water spraying like a crystal fan, and he smiles. I swear to God, he smiles. And then he takes to scanning the horizon again, as he has done all his life, looking for that which makes his heart pound and his throat fill with a soft growl.

At noon, we share a sandwich. Thor and I. He wolfs his share down as he has always done. I eat half of mine and offer him the remaining half. He takes it, giving me a look of gratitude. Or maybe he thinks I'm a dummy, willing to give up such good stuff. Given his age, Thor does not sit and wait for ducks as patiently as when he was younger. So when I let some widgeons and two wood duck hens go by without firing, he snarls at me and pushes at my leg. I forget now what time it was. Late afternoon, I'd guess.

A flock of seven mallards works our decoys. On the second swing, I pick a greenhead and drop it. Thor marks the fall. And, on command, he courses out into the open water and on to the gray buck brush, where he finds the bird and picks it up. And this is where it all happens.

Thor picks up the bird, but instead of coming straight back to me, he heads for the far side of the pothole. Instead of coming directly back to me as he had been trained to do, as he had done countless times over the years, he detours across the lumpy weed growth to a strip of high land. I can see him all the way. And he can see me. But the whole operation takes a minute longer than it should. Finally, he comes to heel, bird in mouth, and I take it from him, but there is no praise.

Why did he take the long route? Was he perhaps squeezing one more moment of ecstasy out of a time that for him was rapidly diminishing? I didn't know anything about all that at the time.

We have our limit of ducks for the day, the two mallards and a wood duck that dropped close to us for an easy retrieve. There is nothing left for the two of us to do except watch the movement of birds and take pleasure from it. The dog stands out at the edge of the marsh grass, belly deep in the water. He stares across the water and he watches the birds and his tail wags and his eyes glisten and his body trembles.

He is wet and he is muddy, and he shivers along the length of his back and into his flanks. The sun is dropping and darkness is about to cover the swamps and we have to get back to the boat because there is yet a long way to go to camp.

I call to Thor. But he does not respond. He stands out in the water looking and watching and shivering and wondering why I do not shoot. So I walk up to my dog on this evening of evenings and I kneel beside him in the water and watch what he is watching. And in that first moment I know what this is all about.

We see ducks working the skyline, circling, talking, and coming in to those places of refuge where they can rest and eat. Beautiful birds. They are the lumber from which eternity is constructed. My dog knows that. And now I know it.

Thor, I discover then, as if I didn't know it before, is smarter than I am. These sights do not come that often in a lifetime. You see them, early on, but you don't really appreciate them. You have to grow old. You have to get really close to death to see sunsets and wild, free ducks as they really are.

That is why my dog did not respond to call, I am sure now. He was sipping from the cup one more time. He was telling me, you see, that he was going to die, that he would never have this opportunity again, and he was going to make the most of it.

And he was right.

I know all about that now, but I was not capable of putting it all together at the time.

We get back to the boat and he jumps in. We get back to the camp. After he eats, I have to lift him up onto the couch where he will spend the night. I will lift him down in the morning.

If you own an old dog and if you work with him and play with him and live with him and forgive him his shortcomings and beg more time for him, you will understand why I wept that night in the duck camp. Thor and I did not hunt together again after that. Some good people salted a field with ring-necks for Thor in December, and we worked them. But it was over. He knew it, and I knew it.

So it came to pass that in July of that next year, Thor went down at thirteen years of age and more miles than you can count. In the end, it makes no difference what anybody else thought about Thor. I knew he was the beginning and the end of everything. I like to believe he thought the same about me.

So give me a day that I can make last forever. No question. Make mine with Thor.

God, how I loved that dog.

CONTRIBUTORS

Sandy Smith, as a reporter for *Time* magazine and a number of Chicago newspapers for more than fifty-eight years, investigated schemes ranging from Mafia plots to Watergate. Retiring in 1997, he returned to his beloved Montana, where, in the 1940s, as an amateur dog trainer and field-trialer, he had crossed paths with the legendary Panther. Always intrigued by the diminutive Labrador's story, he put his reporter's hat back on and began digging into one of field-trialing's best-kept secrets.

Joe Arnette is a former wildlife biologist who, some years ago, "dropped out" in favor of bird hunting, dog training, and writing. He is a columnist and feature writer for a half dozen national magazines, the author of *Gun Dog Chronicles: Reflections on Upland Bird Dogs* and *Waterfowl Retrievers,* the co-author of *Training Spaniels and Retrievers to Hunt 'Em Up,* and the editor of the anthology *A Dog For All Seasons: The Labrador Retriever.*

John Madson wrote about his passion for the outdoors in a wide range of publications, including *Audubon, National Geographic, Reader's Digest,* and in many of the nation's best sporting magazines. The former wildlife biologist's books include *Up on the River, Out Home, Tall Grass Prairie,* and *Where the Sky Began,* among others. Madson died in 1995, but his writings continue to exert an influence on those who share his love for the natural world.

Michael Furtman is a full-time writer whose articles and photographs have appeared in *Ducks Unlimited* magazine, *Wildfowl*, and in many others. He has written thirteen books, including his most recent, *Duck Country*, published by DU. Furtman is the recipient of the Jade of Chiefs Award, the highest conservation honor given by the Outdoor Writers Association of America. He lives in Duluth, Minnesota, with his wife, Mary Jo, and Wigeon, their black Labrador retriever.

Richard E. Massey lives in Minnesota, where he spends his prime time on Lac qui Parle Lake hunting ducks and geese with his sons Jake and Will. He's a high school English teacher, with a keen interest in getting kids involved in hunting, fishing, habitat development, and water quality.

Doug Larsen lives a life inextricably linked to the outdoors. A tireless duck hunter since childhood, he has been a guide on two continents, and his career in sporting travel has afforded him the opportunity to go around the globe in pursuit of waterfowl and other outdoor passions. He lives in western Pennsylvania with his wife, Katie, three kids, and a calamitous pile of duck hunting paraphernalia.

Wade Bourne has owned and hunted over Labrador retrievers for more than thirty years. Bourne is a regular contributor to national outdoor publications, including *Ducks Unlimited* magazine. He hosts the *Pros' Pointers Radio* syndication and *Pros' Pointers TV* segments. He will appear as host of *Ducks Unlimited TV* in 2004, and he is the author of four books, including *DU's Decoys and Proven Methods for Using Them* and *The DU Guide to Hunting Dabblers.* Bourne resides with his wife, two children, and two dogs on their family farm at Clarksville, Tennessee.

Chuck Petrie is the executive editor of *Duck Unlimited* magazine. His articles, essays, and stories have appeared in that publication and in other outdoor magazines. He is the author of the books *Just Retrievers* and *North America's Greatest Waterfowling Lodges & Outfitters*, as well as editor of numerous other titles. An ardent waterfowl hunter and fly-fisherman, he lives in Cordova, Tennessee, with his wife, Mary.

E. Donnall Thomas Jr. writes regularly about the outdoor life for a number of respected publications, including *Gray's Sporting Journal, Alaska, Ducks Unlimited, Big Sky Journal, Shooting Sportsman,* and *Outdoor Life.* His books include *The Life of a Lab, Labs Afield, White Fish Can't Jump, The Double Helix, By Dawn's Early Light, Dream Fish & Road Trips,* and several others. Thomas lives in central Montana with his wife, Lori, four children, and assorted dogs.

Ted Nelson Lundrigan is a country lawyer who loves to wander the hills of his native northern Minnesota, drawing deeply upon the hospitality of those who live there and adding to the idle curiosity of those who don't. He has written two books about grouse hunting, *Hunting the Sun* and *Grouse and Lesser Gods*, and has published a number of stories in magazines such as *Shooting Sportsman,*

Sporting Classics, and *Gun Dog.* He has fought in a war, helped raise four children, and trained four gun dogs.

Mel Ellis was a prolific writer and observer of the Wisconsin landscape. For fifteen years he wrote an outdoor column for *The Milwaukee Journal,* and edited a column for *Field & Stream* for more than a decade. His books include *The Land, Always the Land; Flight of the White Wolf;* and *Notes from Little Lakes,* to name just a few.

Michael McIntosh has written an impressive number of books on fine firearms, natural history, and wildlife art. The list includes *Best Guns, A.H. Fox, The Wildfowl Art of David Maass, Shotguns and Shooting,* and many others. These and scoreless articles published in major sporting magazines have earned him a devoted readership worldwide. McIntosh is the gun-review editor for *Shooting Sportsman* magazine, and a regular contributor to *Sporting Classics, Gun Dog,* and *Wildlife Art.* He lives in South Dakota.

John Barsness was born and raised in Montana, where he lives with his wife, Eileen, and their retriever, Gideon. He is a con-tributing editor of *Field & Stream,* and has written for a number of other national outdoor magazines, including *Outdoor Life, Sports Illustrated, Gray's Sporting Journal,* and *Sports Afield.* His books include *Shotguns for Wingshooting, The Life of the Hunt, Montana Time,* and other titles that cover his broad sporting interests, which range from big-game hunting to fly-fishing.

CONTRIBUTORS

Dan O'Brien has written numerous books of fiction and non-fiction about the West. His most recent book, *Buffalo for the Broken Heart,* explores the conversion of his 3,000-acre South Dakota cattle ranch to a buffalo ranch. Other books by O'Brien include *Equinox, The Rites of Autumn,* and *The Contract Surgeon.* He has worked as an endangered-species biologist and an English teacher. He lives in Whitewood, South Dakota.

John Hewitt, the senior editor of *Gray's Sporting Journal,* is a carpenter in Fairbanks, Alaska. A former Marine officer, he survived Vietnam, he says, by basic good luck. He is also a former big-game guide who quit that venture after eight years because it interfered enormously with his duck hunting.

John R. Wright is the author of the book *Trout on a Stick.* An avid waterfowler, former wrangler and hunting guide, he has written a number of articles for *Ducks Unlimited* magazine and other publications. He lives in Mancos, Colorado.

Jay Reed was for nearly forty years an outdoor writer for the *Milwaukee Journal* and the *Journal Sentinel.* His love of duck hunting and retrievers was well known by his many loyal readers. Reed left high school early, lying about his age to join the Marine Corps during World War II. He was recalled to service again during the Korean War, and covered the Vietnam War as a journalist, becoming a finalist for a Pulitzer Prize. Fittingly, when Reed died in 2002, the headline in the *Milwaukee Journal Sentinel* read: "Jay and his trusty friend, Thor, have gone hunting again."